# THE BEGGAR'S OPERA, Act III

**A Painting by William Hogarth** (*Reproduced by courtesy of the Trustees of the Tate Gallery, London*)

*A performance at Lincoln's Inn Fields, showing the two heroines on their knees (Lucy Lockit to the left and Polly Peachum to the right) pleading with their fathers to save Macheath, who is in irons in New-gate prison. (See Airs 54 and 55.) Among the audience may be seen John Gay directly behind Peachum, Mr. Rich, the producer, in profile to Gay's left, and the Duke of Bolton seated at the far right and gazing at Polly (the reigning stage queen, Miss Fenton) who was later to become the Duchess of Bolton.*

# THE BEGGAR'S OPERA

### BY JOHN GAY

A FAITHFUL REPRODUCTION OF THE
1729 Edition

which includes the WORDS and MUSIC of
all the AIRS, as well as the SCORE for the overture

*With commentaries*
*by* LOUIS KRONENBERGER *and*
MAX GOBERMAN

*on the literary and musical background*
*and with the* ORIGINAL WORDS
*of all the airs that John Gay* ADAPTED *for this work*

ARGONAUT BOOKS, PUBLISHERS, *Larchmont, New York*
MCMLXI

# TABLE OF CONTENTS

# THE BEGGARS OPERA.

*Brittons attend — view this harmonious Stage,*
*And listen to these notes which charm the age.*
*Thus shall your tastes in* Sounds & Sense *be shown,*
*And Beggars Opras ever be your own.*

# *THE BEGGAR'S OPERA*
## BY
## LOUIS KRONENBERGER

I N THE SIXTY-ODD YEARS that separate Farquhar's *The Beaux Stratagem* from Goldsmith's *She Stoops to Conquer* the English stage can boast only one really memorable occasion. *The Beggar's Opera* is still so vivid that we have no trouble grasping why it was memorable: even putting the music to one side, John Gay wrote a far better libretto than any of his contemporaries wrote plays. That he did so must reflect, of course, on the plays. Again, that *The Beggar's Opera*—a medley of borrowed tunes—should have taken London by storm and had an unprecedented run of sixty-three nights, must reflect in a sense on the operas. It does not prove that they were bad, but it does suggest that many of them, for audiences in general, were boring.

The English love music, at least when it is rollicking and rhythmical—something, as Handel told Gluck, that "they can beat time to"; and even more the English love humor, particularly when it is lively and pointed. And here, in the early eighteenth century—when an all-too-notoriously cynical Restoration theatre had left in its wake an all-too-pallidly sentimental one—they had to listen to elegantly florid operas with dismal plots, and sit through comedies often as lacking in blood as they were dripping with tears.

And just then—the year is 1728—Gay came up with *The Beggar's Opera*.

# THE BEGGAR'S OPERA

Seldom has success been greater, or more easily explained. For the great populace of London here was something distinctly new and decidedly congenial. Instead of the weepy plays and the highflown operas, here was the raffish underworld of London, filled with human voices and downright speech. Here, moreover, was hard and downright comedy; here, once again, was satire at the expense of the Prime Minister and his mistress and his wife. In other words here, along with something that crackled, was the sense—for those who might care—of something that scorched and stung. And doubtless more than anything else, here was an arrangement of winning tunes. At one stroke everything that had gone over most Londoners' heads without touching their hearts was banished: at one stroke ballad opera came into its own. No wonder that ladies inscribed the lyrics of *The Beggar's Opera* on their fans and their drawing-room screens; it had them truly in raptures, it was truly the rage.

The amount of audience-impact that *The Beggar's Opera* possessed we can only compute in terms of all the needs that *The Beggar's Opera* managed to satisfy. It was an excellent comedy in an age where good comedy was wanting, an excellent musical comedy in an age that had hardly known such a thing could exist. It told pungent truth on a stage grown torpid with flabby lies; and it used pungent language in an age becoming more and more mealy-mouthed. So much for it in terms of the great gap it filled: it was justly a thundering hit; it is justly, today, a classic. That is not to suggest that *The Beggar's Opera* is a notable work of art. It couldn't be: it is too mixed a thing, born of too momentary intentions. The wonder is that anything so much dedicated to the spirit of the hour—to taking potshots at Sir Robert Walpole, to making lowbrow fun of the fashionable Italian opera, to thrusting a torch into the underworld of London—should prove every bit as durable as a work of art; should be, after some 230 years, as richly entertaining as it is informative.

The best proof of its hardihood is how well it has survived, rather than outlived, its original purposes. Today, for example, few people know, and fewer care, that it held Walpole up to ridicule; it lives on because it equally held the mirror up to Nature. It tells us, on a smaller scale and in a more artificial manner, what Defoe and Fielding and Hogarth tell us—a good deal about the seamy side of the age; and few ages have been endowed with a seamier one. The special satiric point about *The Beggar's Opera*—the point involving Walpole—is much less that there was tremendous poverty in Gay's London, or tremendous crime, than that there was tremendous corruption. It was not the amount of theft that stood out but the amount of bribery; and not that methods were underhand but that people were two-faced. There was no honesty among respectable men, and no honor among thieves. In terms of social history, *The Beggar's Opera* offers us a picturesque and tolerably accurate look at the underworld; in terms of ironic satire, it manages, in the act of portraying the criminal classes, to pillory their betters.

One can thoroughly enjoy *The Beggar's Opera* while knowing nothing of Walpole but one ought, I think, to know of him because he was so interesting a man. Indeed, there have been few men so interesting whom the world has so much ceased to be interested in. Surely one reason for the world's neglect is that Walpole lacks conventional fascination and color. He had no romantic or heroic or demonic qualities of either good or evil; was neither a gaudy swashbuckler nor a plunging buccaneer. In other words, there is not a single drop of poetry in Walpole; he is all prose, all sanity and disillusioned realism, and our final judgment against him is rather that he helped make England a philistine nation of shopkeepers than that, in his own day, he half turned it into an unblushing nation of crooks. He was a very great administrator and knew it, and as he wanted peace and prosperity for England he wanted power for himself. A complete and unblinking realist, an utter and unblushing cynic, he insisted he knew only two ways to govern, by corruption or by force; and he chose corruption. In a certain sense he used corruption as a means rather than an end; in a certain sense he used it as a lesser evil than the sanguinary cabals and conspiracies of Stuart times. In a certain sense, he makes excellent sense; and might indeed have fairly boasted on his tombstone that he kept England out of war, two monarchs on their thrones, and a nation on its feet; as he might have boasted too of being personally a very bluff, open, likeable man.

But the fact remains that he fostered an age that was hideously dishonest about money and outrageously heartless about how that money was gouged out of the poor. The methods of Peachum and Lockit in *The Beggar's Opera* are the methods of every kind of politician and plunderer in the age of Walpole: so much so that if Gay's satire constitutes a direct hit at Walpole, it would have constituted one almost anywhere it landed, for Walpole was simply the commander-in-chief of a great army of mercenaries.

As a direct hit at Walpole's personal life,* with Polly Peachum and Lucy

* It was so direct a one that *Polly*, the sequel to *The Beggar's Opera*, was denied a license.

# THE BEGGAR'S OPERA

Lockit representing the mistress whom Walpole eventually married and the wife he never loved, the triangle story of *The Beggar's Opera* no longer matters and must stand or fall on how good it is as theatre. But it is worth noting that even as the butt of the piece Walpole himself was made generally likeable: Macheath possesses enough of what made Walpole bluff and friendly to become the undoubted hero of *The Beggar's Opera*. The ironic point there, of course, lies in making a hero of a highwayman. But that has less to do with one man's particular nature than with what we might call eternal audience taste; audiences always have a soft spot for adventurous and swaggering bad men, whether highwaymen or pirates or train robbers. It is not the least entertaining aspect of Gay's piece that in satirizing Walpole it also romanticized him, and that he is quite as much brightened in *The Beggar's Opera* as he is blackened.

For that we can be very grateful, for without such a Macheath as Gay provides his Opera might have just as great value as an exposé but would have nothing like so much as entertainment. *The Beggar's Opera* is ballad opera not only for using popular tunes and working at a popular level but for providing much the same plot-appeal as a good ballad does; and something of the same insistent swing. And that swing, which the character and actions of Macheath do more than anything except the music to create, is essential to the vigor of the piece, and indeed works hand-in-glove with, rather than counter to, the satire and the sordidness. Nor is Gay's picture, even in the documentary sense, essentially less truthful for being so raffish and lively. It is the fault of the naturalistic theatre, as it is of the social-worker mind, to coat sordidness with dullness, and not to realize that it is oftener the good people of the world who are bores.

It is a matter of record that the day of their executions brought out, among eighteenth-century criminals, the actor and the exhibitionist in them—that they died with more swagger and glitter than most people live. It is a matter of record again that, while there may be very little honor among thieves there is a tremendous amount of humor; and conceivably out of hoodwinking one another they got a greater satisfaction than out of hoodwinking a credulous public. It is finally a matter of record that eighteenth-century prison life, while unspeakably foul and (for those without money) outrageously brutal, could be—for those who had money and could dish it out to wardens and turnkeys—quite as full of wine, women and song as the life outside. It was the nineteenth-century era of reform that along with its sanitary improvements introduced solitary confinement, and that while reducing the horrors of prison life increased the tedium. The underworld life of the eighteenth century was certainly hideous but it wasn't grim. It was an age when men starved through drinking gin; in other ages men have starved without drinking it.

At any rate, the double philosophy that runs through *The Beggar's Opera*—of dog-eat-dog on the one hand, and on the other of eat, drink and be merry for tomorrow we die on the gallows—seems a genuine reflection of how the underworld of Gay's time felt. We get a feeling not of people possessed by crime but of people choosing crime in preference to hopeless poverty. They would rather have their fun for a while and die on the gallows than have no fun at all and die in the gutter. It is an attitude born less of viciousness than of desperation, as even their betrayal of one another does not so much suggest innate lack of heart as hearts that have gradually hardened. It is not for reasons of snobbery that the Peachums don't want Polly to marry a highwayman; it is for reasons of safety. Everywhere there is a dog-eat-dog world where he who sentimentalizes is lost. It is also a world where, in the end, every one is lost; and in that sense it is something of a melancholy world, but not at all a gloomy one. It is gay rather than gloomy, vivid rather than drab, cold-blooded and horrifying no doubt, but rich in humor. Half a century later Robert Burns was to paint, in shorter span, an even more depraved and bestial picture, and to mingle worse squalor with richer humor, in *The Jolly Beggars*. The note there is more lyrical, as the philosophy is more militant: Burns' sorry figures exult in a life that Gay's merely acquiesce in.

Gay's refusal to be sanctimonious about his characters is one reason why *The Beggar's Opera* has its particular light-hearted swing, and why it remains a satire and not a sermon, a ballad and not a tract. Yet we cannot doubt that, though he refused to preach, Gay in some sense meant his piece for a protest as well as an exposé; meant to reveal the results as well as the methods of wholesale corruption. Indeed Frank Kidson, in writing of *The Beggar's Opera*, was probably right in arguing that Gay's satire at the expense of Walpole has been over-stressed, and that it was the actual rather than the symbolic picture, the criminal world rather than the arch-corrupter, that inspired his opera. Today, at any rate, we certainly need not read the Walpole side of things into the picture, while we simply cannot leave the underworld of Gay's time out of it. And probably no one in Gay's time could either; to Gay's contemporaries Macheath would more readily suggest Jack Sheppard than—for all the references to Bluff Bob or Bob Booty—Sir Robert Walpole; while Peachum's *actual* prototype was at least as much Fielding's Jonathan Wild—that great coldblooded gangleader who squealed on his own men before they could squeal on him, and informed on other men because they would not join his gang—as it was Walpole's brother-in-law Townshend.

All this, in any case, is obvious material for satire and exposé, as it is first-rate stuff for entertainment. Or for those, at least, who find raffishness and unrespectability entertaining: there must always be people who take genteel umbrage at Villon's Paris or Dekker's London or Burns' Scotland or Aristophanes' Greece, and who will find Gay's "Newgate pastoral" as shocking in its manifold duplicities as it is sordid in its unvarnished details. And in terms of what is harsh about *The Beggar's Opera* there was one aspect that perhaps was new and that makes it exhilarating today. That aspect is the professionalism, the matter-of-factness, at times the ironically intended self-righteousness of many of its characters. When they discuss their particular life and their particular world, they aren't talking crime, they are talking shop. And just as Macheath is the outlaw hero of the piece, Peachum, as William Empson suggests, is its bourgeois villain. Peachum treats of murder from the same hard-headed business point of view that a real-estate man might treat of mortgages. "Murder," he says, "is as *fashionable* a crime as a man can be guilty of . . . If they have wherewithal to persuade the Jury to bring it in manslaughter, what are they the worse for it?" He discusses Macheath's qualifications as a husband much as any worldly man might discuss a son-in-law: "Besides what he hath already, I know he is in a fair way of getting, or of dying; and both these ways, let me tell you, are most excellent chances for a wife." There is more than piquancy to such an attitude; there is cutting irony: this *kind* of reasoning is just as characteristic of the middle class as of the criminal class. And indeed a criminal's way of making a living can be easily identified with a respectable man's. Says Peachum:

> A Lawyer is an honest Employment, so is mine. Like me too he acts in
> a double capacity, both against Rogues and for 'em; for 'tis but fitting
> that we should protect and encourage Cheats, since we live by 'em.

Less often Gay turns directly satirical, though the analogy between crooks operating in the underworld and politicians in the great world is time and again to be inferred. "In one respect indeed," Peachum says straight out, "our employment may be reckon'd dishonest, because, like Great Statesmen, we encourage those who betray their friends." Indeed, the final joke, the ultimate ironic slap, is to suggest that, under certain circumstances, the poor may be *almost* as wicked as the powerful. "Had the Play remain'd, as I at first intended," says the Beggar just before the final curtain, "it would have carried a most excellent moral. 'Twould have shown that the lower sort of people have *their* vices in a degree as well as the rich: and that they are punish'd for them." That is an admirable touch: it says just what Gay wanted said; and being said, it lets him wind up his *Opera* with the sudden and charming shamelessness, the happy ending to mock all happy endings, that so nicely consorts with its tone and mood: "The catastrophe," says the Player, on hearing that Macheath is to be hanged, "is manifestly wrong, for an Opera must end happily." And the Beggar replies: "Your Objection, Sir, is very just; and is easily remov'd. So," he calls out, "you rabble there—run and cry a Reprieve—let the prisoner be brought back to his wives in triumph." "All this," concludes the Player, "we must do, to comply with the taste of the town."

For the tunes that Gay found in the popular musical literature, he supplied (while occasionally retaining a phrase or refrain) apposite new lyrics of his own. Few of them are brilliant, and the least of them are doggerel, but besides fitting the music they often very well fit the action, further the satire, or point up the theme:

> *Thus Gamesters united in friendship are found,*
> *Though they know that their industry all is a cheat;*
> *They flock to their prey at the Dice-box's sound,*
> *And join to promote one another's deceit.*
> > *But if by mishap*
> > *They fail of a chap,*
> *To keep in their hands, they each other entrap.*
> *Like Pikes, lank with hunger, who miss of their ends,*
> *They bite their companions, and prey on their friends.*

The lyrics add, with a bounce and bite of their own, just what is required to go with Gay's notably right and robust libretto—one of the very few librettos that can stand happily on their own feet. But this in the end is an "Opera"; and how much better it is when those feet have been set to dancing; when Gay's lyrics are not recited but sung; when, as it were, Orpheus descends once again to the Underworld.

*XIII*

# THE MUSIC OF *The Beggar's Opera*

## BY

## MAX GOBERMAN

To SAVOR FULLY the delight which greeted John Gay's score for *The Beggar's Opera* in the London of 1728, one must be acquainted with the musical stance of the time. England's "golden age of music" had come to a close with the death of that beloved genius Henry Purcell in 1695. This had been the period of great English opera, of chests of viols in the home, of coffee clubs for singing catches and rounds, of quiet contemplative music in the "fantasia manner". Roger North in *The Musicall Grammarian* said of this period: ". . . . music flourished and exceedingly improved . . . held up her head . . . in private society, for many chose rather to fiddle at home than to go out and be knocked on the head abroad. . . .".

This healthy musical life started to crumble with the advent in 1660 of Charles II, who applied his recently acquired French taste in music by setting up a band of fiddlers in slavish imitation of the "vingt-quatre violons du roy" of the French king. He was reputed to have liked only that music to which he could beat time (easily, one supposes). High in Charles' favor was a French musician, Louis Grabu, who had accompanied his royal master to England, where he wrote *Albion and Albanius, an Opera, or Representation in Musick* with words by John Dryden. Although Dryden spoke highly of Grabu in the preface —he later showed better taste in doing the same for Purcell—the piece was a worthless one.

At the same time, opera was becoming a flourishing institution in Italy.

With the stage set by the English court for all sorts of entertainment, Italian opera made its first appearance in England in 1705. Thomas Clayton, a member of the King's band who had studied in Italy and had some knowledge of the Italian opera method, brought back some operatic songs and, with the aid of one Peter Motteux, whipped up a plot of sorts, translated the songs into English, and staged the concoction under the title *Arsinoe, Queen of Cyprus*. It was performed at Drury Lane with the best English singers. It ran for 24 nights in the first season and 11 in the next. All writers of the time agreed that it was a contemptible work as regards both words and music.

There followed a spate of bad works from which England never recovered. One of these, for example, was an opera called *Pyrrhus and Demetrius* with music by Alessandro Scarlatti. It was sung half in English and half in Italian. Richard Steele wrote of it in the *Tatler*: ". . . a great critic fell into fits in the gallery at feeling, not only time and place, but language and nations confused in the most incorrigible manner. . . .". Addison, in the *Spectator*, said: "There is no question but our great-grandchildren will be very curious to know the reason why their forefathers used to sit together like an audience of foreigners in their own country to hear whole plays acted before them in a tongue which they did not understand. In short, our English music is quite rooted out, and nothing yet planted in its stead."

Not only was English music rooted out but, as the craze grew, the English performers who had started the first Italian opera on its way were replaced by imported prima donnas and castrati and were rendered completely unemployed. John Gay wrote Swift in 1723: "There's nobody allowed to say, I sing, but an eunuch or an Italian woman." Referring to Senesino, a castrato, later in the same letter, Gay says he "daily is voted to be the greatest man that ever lived." Much savage humor attended this craze on the part of the upper classes. One writer, after listening to an Italian opera translated into English, said he had never heard so many notes and so much music devoted to extolling the glories of the definite article. Another slyly suggested that the gallants in the audience found the program impossible to read in English, that it had to be translated into Italian. One thing was sure—nonsense on the stage, accompanied by florid music, reigned supreme.

Into this situation came one of the world's truly great composers, the Saxon Georg Friedrich Händel (later anglicized to George Frederick Handel). He arrived in England in 1710 with no particular thought of settling there.

# THE BEGGAR'S OPERA

Aaron Hill, manager of the Haymarket Theatre, prevailed upon him to write an opera for his theatre. That opera was *Rinaldo*, from which John Gay was later to borrow the march that became even more famous as "Let us take the road" (Air XX in *The Beggar's Opera*).

John Walsh, publisher of the opera, is said to have made a profit of fifteen hundred pounds on it. Handel is purported to have proposed as a result of this, "You shall compose the next opera and I will publish it." *Rinaldo* was the first of some thirty-odd operas which Handel composed, borrowed and stole in the accepted style of the day. Who of us has escaped the so-called "Largo" from *Xerxes* by Handel? But how many of us know that it comes from an Italian opera, *Serse*, first produced in London?

But while the Italian opera had its devoted following of courtiers, the lower classes never really took to it. When the word spread in January of 1728 that a new "ballad opera" had appeared, with a score made mainly out of well-known folk songs whose words were already widely familiar, a large and eager audience was ready to receive it with immediate, resounding and long-lasting acclaim.

Six months after *The Beggar's Opera* was first performed, Handel's Royal Academy opera company ended its ninth, and last, season under a large deficit. Italian opera never recovered from the blow dealt by Gay's impudent work. It is a commentary on the great inner calm of Handel that three years later he nevertheless performed his *Acis and Galatea*, composed in 1720—with a text by John Gay.

The immediate predecessor of *The Beggar's Opera* was *The Gentle Shepherd* by Allan Ramsay, poet, wigmaker and bookseller. This ballad opera was in rhyme, with short separate songs adapted to well-known Scotch tunes, and bore the subtitle "A pastoral comedy". Gay evidently discussed this work with Swift, for Pope wrote: "Dr. Swift had been observing once to Mr. Gay what an odd pretty sort of thing a Newgate Pastoral might make". Since Gay had a wide knowledge of the songs of the day (he was also supposed to be something of a flutist), the suggestion fell in fertile ground.

The songs used by Gay range from simple folk ditties to quite sophisticated art songs by Purcell and others. Gay fitted them out with new words, at times retaining key phrases from the originals, at other times utilizing completely new ideas. (See page xxv for a detailed comparison of Gay's verses with the originals.)

Almost all—and there are many—of the Scotch songs in *The Beggar's Opera* are to be found in William Thomson's *Orpheus Caledonius*. Gay's patroness, the Scottish Duchess of Queensberry, was a subscriber to Thomson's collection for three copies, and Gay undoubtedly took this opportunity to become familiar with these great songs.

The chief source of the songs in *The Beggar's Opera* was Thomas D'Urfey's *Wit and Mirth: Or Pills to Purge Melancholy*, edited originally by Henry Playford. Gay undoubtedly knew the work in its final six-volume edition published 1719-20. The immediate progenitor of this superb collection was a drollery entitled *An Antidote against Melancholy*, published by Henry Playford's father, John, in 1661.

Tom D'Urfey, with his long nose, his bass voice, and his impudent vulgar wit, was the indispensable entertainer of the gentry and nobility for nearly forty years. "The Town may da-da-damn me for a Poet, but they si-si-sing my songs for all that". (D'Urfey stuttered except when singing or swearing.) Charles II was a great admirer of D'Urfey and his innumerable songs. He was so charmed, for example, by little Molly Davis' singing of "My lodging it is on the cold ground" that it is said he "Rais'd her from her Bed on the Cold Ground to a Bed Royal". "I myself," Addison remarked in 1713, "remember King Charles the Second leaning on Tom D'Urfey's Shoulder more than once, and humming over a Song with him". Fielding's Squire Western, to borrow an example from fiction, had his daughter play two songs from D'Urfey's *Pills* on the harpsichord every afternoon "as soon as he was drunk". Her personal preference, since she was a young lady of refined taste, was for the compositions of Mr. Handel. The use of many of D'Urfey's songs in *The Beggar's Opera* did much to make them respectable.

Imagine the delight of the audience when they heard those sturdy, familiar, often beautiful, tunes. Imagine the further pleasure of knowing the words which were being parodied so fittingly, and were sung onstage so well, and in English too.

The songs were originally intended to be sung without any accompaniment, which may explain why they come directly out of the spoken lines with no time allowed for musical introduction to set key or mood. John Rich, manager of the Lincoln's Inn Fields Theatre and original (reputedly unwilling) producer of the opera, suggested at the rehearsal before last that orchestral accompaniments be provided. Some of Gay's friends agreed with the idea, and it was probably at this point that Johann Christoph (John Christopher) Pepusch was called in and asked to do the necessary musical chores.

Pepusch was the son of the minister of a Protestant congregation in Berlin. He emigrated to London in 1700, at the age of 33, and was engaged in the orchestra at Drury Lane. He was a specialist in ancient music, in which he took a deep interest throughout his life. In 1713 he took the degree of Doctor of Music at Oxford, and soon afterwards became musical director of John Rich's theatre, where he remained for many years. In 1724 he was involved in a scheme for starting a college in the Bermudas, and actually embarked— but his ship was wrecked, and he returned to England, probably to his original post.

Pepusch is generally credited with "composing" *The Beggar's Opera*. He did indeed compose the overture, which is in the French style and is wittily contrapuntal while at the same time quoting Lucy's song "I'm like a Skiff on the Ocean tost" (Air XLVII). He probably also wrote out the parts for the musicians, using the basses which appear in this edition. But there is no evidence that he even helped Gay select the tunes.

A curious fact about the score is its subsequent impact on music. For a score so lacking in musical originality (it has been described as a score that one whistles going *into* the theatre) its effects have been singularly far-reaching. It has been suggested that without the "Ballad Opera" by John Gay, there would have been no "Singspiele"—*The Magic Flute* by Mozart, for example.

In keeping with the paradoxical character of *The Beggar's Opera*, with its upside-down morality, further effects of this "unoriginal" score are seen in the constant use of the music up to the present day. Darius Milhaud, for example, arranged Gay's score for his *Opera des Gueux*.

Most ironic of all is that such a work should have been written by a distinctly minor poet who was content to be a kind of hanger-on to the more wealthy and more talented of his generation—and to use on his greatest work the motto:

*Nos haec novissimus esse nihil*
(We know this to be nothing.)

# A Note on *JOHN GAY'S* LIFE

BY

REGINA BARNES

JOHN GAY caught the coattail of immortality with *The Beggar's Opera*. None of his other works could have accomplished this for him, although some were popularly received in his day and remain interesting reflections of early eighteenth-century London and country life.

A country boy, John Gay was born in 1685 of genteel family in the small Devonshire town of Barnstaple, but was orphaned at an early age. After completion of the local, but thorough, grammar school and a brief period of apprenticeship to a silk mercer, the youth made his way to London, where he arrived in 1706 with a small patrimony and a fund of talent.

From his very first appearance in the taverns, his keen wit and uncommonly sweet disposition endeared him to the writers and wits who gathered there. In a comparatively short time Gay, the unknown, became part of the charmed circle which included such men as Pope, Swift, Congreve, Prior, Parnell, Addison, and Arbuthnot. However, according to Dr. Johnson, the affection which his friends bestowed upon Gay was greater than their respect. For he was a born dependent. His capacity for leaning was as unflagging as his ability to gratify those who eventually adopted him either as colleague or household pet.

Gay's fortunes did not prosper as easily as his friendships. Thanks to the initial efforts of Pope and Swift, he secured a series of socially comfortable positions in the homes of the aristocracy. The Duchess of Monmouth, Lord Clarendon, the Earl of Burlington, Mrs. Howard, the Countess of Suffolk, the Duke and Duchess of Queensberry, even Queen Caroline herself, all knew, admired and helped him in various stages of his life.

These relationships as secretary-companion and perpetual guest accustomed Gay to plush comforts and high-caloried tables. But there was little financial security in these posts and he was constantly out of funds. Neither his own writings nor his varying positions could yield enough to keep up with his extravagant desires for the best wines or softest linens. He complained to Swift at one time: "I lodge at Burlington House and have received many civilities from many great men. They wonder at each other at not providing for me, and I wonder at them all."

On the literary front, the battle for recognition was complicated and intense, resulting frequently in lifetime enmities or friendships. Success was to be achieved not only through superior ability but often by fortuitous alliances with powerful patrons of the arts. Gay's dedication to Pope of the poem *Rural Sports* in 1713, and the writing of the successful *The Shepherd's Week*, a pastoral, in support of his friend's position against a rival poet, Ambrose Philips, gained him the lasting devotion of "the wasp of Twickenham". One of the zigzagging literary and political disputes in which Gay became involved eventually mushroomed into his satirization of Walpole.

The goal of monetary success rose and dipped tantalizingly. But in 1720, Gay came into a neat sum with the publication of his *Poems for Several Occasions*. Despite the urgings of his friends that he invest soundly to be "sure of a clean shirt and a shoulder of mutton each day," he chose to sink all in the South Sea Company, a fantastic, speculative venture which held London enthralled. When the "Bubble" collapsed, the poet was ruined. The foundations of the country's economy shook perilously; so did Gay's health. However, his friends rallied uncensoriously around him and, with much diligent care, restored his equanimity.

In 1723, Gay achieved a less brilliant, but far steadier, coup by obtaining the post of Commissioner of Lottery, for £150 a year and a residency in Whitehall. A later appointment, however, as Gentleman Usher to the infant Princess Louisa of the royal household so chagrined him because of its slight dignity that he turned down the £200 a year it brought and left the security of the Court forever.

Like some of the characters he was to create in *The Beggar's Opera*, Gay sniffed the perfumes of the rich but inhaled the sour smells of the poor. The bawdy night life of London drew him irresistibly. Long evenings found him stalking through the teeming, dangerous streets, carousing in shady taverns, frequenting the houses of ill fame, listening to the shrieks and songs of the alleys. He became the acquaintance and recorder of pickpockets, desperadoes and prostitutes. In his plays *The Mohocks, The What D'Ye Call It*, and *The Beggar's Opera*, as in the well-known *Trivia, or The Art of Walking the Streets of London*, Gay portrayed the lower depths of London as indelibly as did his contemporary Hogarth, the painter. His purpose, however, was not to declaim or cry reform. He was temperamentally and artistically unsuited for the pulpit. Rather, his accurate mockery aroused laughter, and, in many, thoughtful praise.

In 1724, caught up in the popular hysteria aroused by the fantastic exploits of one Joseph Blake, an egregious outlaw, Gay wrote the *Newgate Garland*, a ballad in which he depicted the felon as a romantic highwayman.

*The Beggar's Opera* appeared in 1728. So great was its immediate popular appeal that Dr. Herring, an important cleric, appalled by the seductiveness of its vice, thundered against the play in his sermons. This indictment only added to the financial success of the play which, according to a popular *bon mot* of the time, had made Gay rich and Rich (the producer) gay.

*Polly*, a sequel, was written the following year. The play was banned from the boards by Walpole, still smarting from the successful satire leveled against him in *The Beggar's Opera*. There was no prohibition, however, against the publishing of the work, and *Polly* enjoyed the popularity of the censored.

The contradictions latent in Gay's life now became ironically sharp. He had finally achieved wealth, despite political disappointment—yet his devoted friends, the Duke and Duchess of Queensberry, whose household he joined in 1729, lovingly budgeted his money to the point of exacerbating frugality. He remained a bachelor—in the face of genuine affection towards women which he had expressed in lilting songs and tender relationships. Although Gay considered himself essentially a non-political being, Arbuthnot could write jestingly: "He is now become one of the obstructors of the peace of Europe, the terror of the ministry, the author . . . of all the seditious pamphlets against the government. . . ." He was a minor literary figure who, with one play, destroyed the vogue of the Italian Opera in England and substituted a native form which has delighted playgoers to this very day.

However, from the publication of *Polly*, in 1729, to his death three years later, Gay wrote little of consequence. He seemed drained of the spasmodic energy he had formerly possessed and was plagued with recurrent bouts of colic. In March of 1732, Gay wrote to Swift: "I find myself dispirited for want of having some pursuit . . . I begin to find a dislike of society . . . ." By December of that year he was dead, having succumbed to a violent attack of colic. Characteristically, he left no will. His two widowed sisters inherited his estate, variously estimated at between three thousand and six thousand pounds.

John Gay was buried in Westminster Abbey near the tomb of Chaucer. Pope's epitaph is engraved on his monument, erected by the Duke and Duchess of Queensberry:

> *Of manners gentle, of affections mild;*
> *In wit a man—simplicity, a child;*
> *With native humour temp'ring virtuous rage;*
> *Form'd to delight at once and lash the age . . .*
>
> *These are thy honours, not that here thy bust*
> *Is mixed with heroes, or with kings thy dust;*
> *But that the worthy and the good shall say,*
> *Striking their pensive bosoms, 'Here lies Gay.'*

To this must be added Gay's own couplet, which he had instructed should be carved on his stone:

> *Life is a jest, and all things show it,*
> *I thought so once, but now I know it.*

# THE MAJOR WORKS OF JOHN GAY

| 1708 | WINE—*poetry* |
| 1712 | THE MOHOCKS—*play* |
| 1713 | RURAL SPORTS—*poetry* |
| | THE WIFE OF BATH—*play* |
| | THE FAN—*poetry* |
| 1714 | THE SHEPHERD'S WEEK—*poetry* |
| | A LETTER TO A LADY—*poetry* |
| 1715 | THE WHAT D'YE CALL IT—*play* |
| 1716 | TRIVIA, OR THE ART OF WALKING THE STREETS OF LONDON—*poetry* |
| 1717 | THREE HOURS AFTER MARRIAGE—*play* |
| 1720 | POEMS ON SEVERAL OCCASIONS—*poetry* |
| 1724 | THE CAPTIVES—*play* |
| 1727 | FABLES—*poetry* |
| 1728 | THE BEGGAR'S OPERA—*play* |
| 1729 | POLLY—*play* |
| 1730 | THE WIFE OF BATH—*revised* |
| 1732 | ACIS AND GALATEA—*Libretto for the opera by Handel* |

PUBLISHED POSTHUMOUSLY:

| 1733 | ACHILLES—*play* |
| 1734 | THE DISTRESSED WIFE—*play* |
| 1738 | FABLES—*a second edition* |
| 1754 | THE REHEARSAL AT GOATHAM—*play* |

# THE
# BEGGAR's
# OPERA.

As it is Acted at the

## THEATRE-ROYAL

IN

## LINCOLNS-INN FIELDS.

Written by Mr. *GAY.*

———— *Nos hæc noviſſimus eſſe nihil.*  Mart.

The THIRD EDITION:
With the OUVERTURE in SCORE,
*The* SONGS, *and the* BASSES,
(The OUVERTURE and BASSES Compos'd by Dr. *PEPUSCH*)
*Curiouſly Engrav'd on* COPPER PLATES.

*LONDON:*
Printed for JOHN WATTS, at the Printing-Office in *Wild-Court*, near *Lincoln's-Inn Fields.*
MDCCXXIX.

A

# TABLE of the SONGS.

## ACT I.

A 2　　　　　　　　　　　　　　　AIR 12.

# A TABLE of the AIRS.

# A TABLE of the AIRS.

Dramatis

# Dramatis Personæ.

## M E N.

Peachum.                               Mr. *Hippefley.*
Lockit.                                Mr. *Hall.*
Macheath.                              Mr. *Walker.*
Filch.                                 Mr. *Clark.*
Jemmy Twitcher.                        Mr. *H. Bullock.*
*Crook-finger'd* Jack.                 Mr. *Houghton.*
Wat Dreary.                            Mr. *Smith.*
Robin *of* Bagfhot.   } *Macheath's* Gang.   Mr. *Lacy.*
*Nimming* Ned.                         Mr. *Pit.*
Harry Padington.                       Mr. *Eaton.*
Mat *of the* Mint.                     Mr. *Spiller.*
Ben Budge.                             Mr. *Morgan.*
*Beggar.*                              Mr. *Chapman.*
*Player.*                              Mr. *Milward.*

*Conftables, Drawer, Turnkey,* &c.

## W O M E N.

*Mrs.* Peachum.                        Mrs. *Martin.*
Polly Peachum.                         Mifs *Fenton.*
Lucy Lockit.                           Mrs. *Egleton.*
Diana Trapes.                          Mrs. *Martin.*
*Mrs.* Coaxer.                         Mrs. *Holiday.*
Dolly Trull.                           Mrs. *Lacy.*
*Mrs.* Vixen.                          Mrs. *Rice.*
Betty Doxy.           } *Women of the Town.*   Mrs. *Rogers.*
Jenny Diver.                           Mrs. *Clarke.*
*Mrs.* Slammekin.                      Mrs. *Morgan.*
Suky Tawdry.                           Mrs. *Palin.*
Molly Brazen.                          Mrs. *Sallee.*

I N T R O-

# INTRODUCTION.

## *BEGGAR. PLAYER.*

### BEGGAR.

F Poverty be a title to Poetry, I am fure no-body can difpute mine. I own my-felf of the company of Beggars; and I make one at their weekly feftivals at St. *Giles*'s. I have a fmall yearly Salary for my Catches, and am welcome to a din-ner there whenever I pleafe, which is more than moft Poets can fay.

*Player.* As we live by the Mufes, 'tis but gratitude in us to encourage poetical merit where-ever we find it. The Mufes, contrary to all other ladies, pay no diftinction to drefs, and never partially miftake the pertnefs of embroi-dery for wit, nor the modefty of want for dulnefs. Be the author who he will, we pufh his Play as far as it will go. So (though you are in want) I wifh you fuccefs heartily.

*Beggar.*

*Beggar.* This piece I own was originally writ for the celebrating the marriage of *James Chanter* and *Moll Lay,* two most excellent ballad-singers. I have introduc'd the Similes that are in all your celebrated *Operas:* The *Swallow,* the *Moth,* the *Bee,* the *Ship,* the *Flower,* &c. Besides, I have a prison Scene, which the ladies always reckon charmingly pathetick. As to the parts, I have observ'd such a nice impartiality to our two ladies, that it is impossible for either of them to take offence. I hope I may be forgiven, that I have not made my Opera throughout unnatural, like those in vogue; for I have no Recitative : excepting this, as I have consented to have neither Prologue nor Epilogue, it must be allow'd an Opera in all its forms. The piece indeed hath been heretofore frequently represented by ourselves in our great room at St. *Giles*'s, so that I cannot too often acknowledge your charity in bringing it now on the Stage.

*Player.* But I see 'tis time for us to withdraw ; the Actors are preparing to begin. Play away the Ouverture. *[Exeunt.*

The

# THE
# *BEGGAR's* OPERA.

## ACT I. SCENE I.

### SCENE Peachum's *House*.

*Peachum sitting at a Table with a large Book of Accounts before him.*

AIR I. An old woman cloathed in gray.

*T*HROUGH all the employments of life
    *Each neighbour abuses his brother;*
*Whore and Rogue they call Husband and Wife:*
    *All professions be-rogue one another.*
*The Priest calls the Lawyer a cheat,*
    *The Lawyer be-knaves the Divine;*
*And the Statesman, because he's so great,*
    *Thinks his trade as honest as mine.*

A Lawyer is an honest employment, so is mine. Like me too he acts in a double capacity, both against Rogues and for 'em; for 'tis but fitting that we should protect and encourage Cheats, since we live by 'em.

B               SCENE

## SCENE II.

### *PEACHUM, FILCH.*

*Filch.* Sir, black *Moll* hath sent word her tryal comes on in the afternoon, and she hopes you will order matters so as to bring her off.

*Peach.* Why, she may plead her belly at worst; to my knowledge she hath taken care of that security. But as the wench is very active and industrious, you may satisfy her that I'll soften the evidence.

*Filch.* *Tom Gagg*, Sir, is found guilty.

*Peach.* A lazy dog! When I took him the time before, I told him what he would come to if he did not mend his hand. This is death without reprieve. I may venture to book him. [*writes.*] For *Tom Gag*, forty pounds. Let *Betty Sly* know that I'll save her from Transportation, for I can get more by her staying in *England*.

*Filch.* *Betty* hath brought more goods into our Lock to-year than any five of the gang; and in truth, 'tis a pity to lose so good a customer.

*Peach.* If none of the gang take her off, she may, in the common course of business, live a twelve-month longer. I love to let women scape. A good sportsman always lets the Hen-Partridges fly, because the breed of the game depends upon them. Besides, here the Law allows us no reward; there is nothing to be got by the death of women ———— except our wives.

*Filch.* Without dispute, she is a fine woman! 'Twas to her I was oblig'd for my education, and (to say a bold word) she hath train'd up more young fellows to the business than the Gaming-table.

*Peach.* Truly, *Filch*, thy observation is right. We and the Surgeons are more beholden to women than all the professions besides.

### A I R II.    The bonny gray-ey'd morn, &c.

*Filch.* '*Tis woman that seduces all mankind,*
    *By her we first were taught the wheedling arts:*
  *Her very eyes can cheat; when most she's kind,*
    *She tricks us of our money with our hearts.*
  *For her, like Wolves by night we roam for prey,*
    *And practise ev'ry fraud to bribe her charms;*
  *For suits of love, like law, are won by pay,*
    *And Beauty must be fee'd into our arms.*

*Peach.*

*Peach.* But make hafte to *Newgate*, boy, and let my friends know what I intend; for I love to make them eafy one way or other.

*Filch.* When a gentleman is long kept in fufpence, penitence may break his fpirit ever after. Befides, certainty gives a man a good air upon his tryal, and makes him rifque another without fear or fcruple. But I'll away, for 'tis a pleafure to be the meffenger of comfort to friends in affliction.

## SCENE III.

### *P E A C H U M.*

But 'tis now high time to look about me for a decent Execution againft next Seffions. I hate a lazy rogue, by whom one can get nothing 'till he is hang'd. A Regifter of the Gang. [*reading.*] Crookfinger'd *Jack.* A year and a half in the fervice: Let me fee how much the ftock owes to his induftry; one, two, three, four, five gold Watches, and feven filver ones. A mighty clean-handed fellow! fixteen Snuff-boxes, five of them of true gold. Six dozen of Handkerchiefs, four filver-hilted Swords, half a dozen of Shirts, three Tye-perriwigs, and a piece of Broad Cloth. Confidering thefe are only the fruits of his leifure hours, I don't know a prettier fellow, for no man alive hath a more engaging prefence of mind upon the road. *Wat Dreary,* alias *Brown Will,* an irregular dog, who hath an underhand way of difpofing of his goods. I'll try him only for a Seffions or two longer upon his good behaviour. *Harry Padington,* a poor petty-larceny rafcal, without the leaft genius; that fellow, though he were to live thefe fix months, will never come to the gallows with any credit. Slippery *Sam*; he goes off the next Seffions, for the villain hath the impudence to have views of following his trade as a Taylor, which he calls an honeft employment. *Mat* of the *Mint*; lifted not above a month ago, a promifing fturdy fellow, and diligent in his way; fomewhat too bold and hafty, and may raife good contributions on the publick, if he does not cut himfelf fhort by murder. *Tom Tipple,* a guzzling foaking fot, who is always too drunk to ftand himfelf, or to make others ftand. A cart is abfolutely neceffary for him. *Robin* of *Bagfhot,* alias *Gorgon,* alias *Bluff Bob,* alias *Carbuncle,* alias *Bob Booty.*

B 2

## SCENE IV.

*PEACHUM*, Mrs. *PEACHUM*.

*Mrs. Peach.* What of *Bob Booty*, husband? I hope nothing bad hath betided him. You know, my dear, he's a favourite cuſtomer of mine. 'Twas he made me a preſent of this ring.

*Peach.* I have ſet his name down in the black-liſt, that's all, my dear; he ſpends his life among women, and as ſoon as his money is gone, one or other of the ladies will hang him for the reward, and there's forty pound loſt to us for-ever.

*Mrs. Peach.* You know, my dear, I never meddle in matters of Death; I always leave thoſe affairs to you. Women indeed are bitter bad judges in theſe caſes, for they are ſo partial to the brave that they think every man handſome who is going to the Camp or the Gallows.

### AIR III.   Cold and raw, &c.

*If any wench* Venus's *girdle wear,*
  *Though ſhe be never ſo ugly,*
*Lillies and roſes will quickly appear,*
  *And her face look wond'rous ſmuggly.*
*Beneath the left ear ſo fit but a cord,*
  *(A rope ſo charming a Zone is!)*
*The youth in his cart hath the air of a lord,*
  *And we cry, There dies an* Adonis!

But really, husband, you ſhould not be too hard-hearted, for you never had a finer, braver ſet of men than at preſent. We have not had a murder among them all, theſe ſeven months. And truly, my dear, that is a great bleſſing.

*Peach.* What a dickens is the woman always a whimpring about murder for? No gentleman is ever look'd upon the worſe for killing a man in his own defence; and if buſineſs cannot be carried on without it, what would you have a gentleman do?

*Mrs. Peach.* If I am in the wrong, my dear, you muſt excuſe me, for no-body can help the frailty of an over-ſcrupulous Conſcience. *Peach.*

*Peach.* Murder is as fashionable a crime as a man can be guilty of. How many fine gentlemen have we in *Newgate* every year, purely upon that article? If they have wherewithal to perfwade the Jury to bring it in manflaughter, what are they the worfe for it? So, my dear, have done upon this fubject. Was captain *Macheath* here this morning, for the bank-notes he left with you laft week?

*Mrs. Peach.* Yes, my dear; and though the Bank hath ftopt payment, he was fo cheerful and fo agreeable! Sure there is not a finer gentleman upon the road than the Captain! If he comes from *Bagfhot* at any reafonable hour he hath promis'd to make one this evening with *Polly*, and me, and *Bob Booty*, at a party of Quadrille. Pray, my dear, is the Captain rich?

*Peach.* The Captain keeps too good company ever to grow rich. *Marybone* and the Chocolate-houfes are his undoing. The man that propofes to get money by play fhould have the education of a fine gentleman, and be train'd up to it from his youth.

*Mrs. Peach.* Really, I am forry upon *Polly*'s account the Captain hath not more difcretion. What bufinefs hath he to keep company with lords and gentlemen? he fhould leave them to prey upon one another.

*Peach.* Upon *Polly*'s account! What, a plague, does the woman mean?--- Upon *Polly*'s account!

*Mrs. Peach.* Captain *Macheath* is very fond of the girl.

*Peach.* And what then?

*Mrs. Peach.* If I have any skill in the ways of women, I am fure *Polly* thinks him a very pretty man.

*Peach.* And what then? you would not be fo mad to have the wench marry him! Gamefters and highwaymen are generally very good to their whores, but they are very devils to their wives.

*Mrs. Peach.* But if *Polly* fhould be in love, how fhould we help her, or how can fhe help herfelf? Poor girl, I am in the utmoft concern about her.

AIR IV.   Why is your faithful flave difdain'd?

> *If love the virgin's heart invade,*
> *How, like a Moth, the fimple maid*
>     *Still plays about the flame!*
> *If foon fhe be not made a wife,*
> *Her honour's fing'd, and then for life,*
>     *She's----what I dare not name.*

*Peach.*

*Peach.* Look ye, wife. A handſome wench in our way of buſineſs is as profitable as at the bar of a *Temple* coffee-houſe, who looks upon it as her livelihood to grant every liberty but one. You ſee I would indulge the girl as far as prudently we can. In any thing, but marriage! after that, my dear, how ſhall we be ſafe? are we not then in her huſband's power? for a huſband hath the abſolute power over all a wife's ſecrets but her own. If the girl had the diſcretion of a court lady, who can have a dozen young fellows at her ear without complying with one, I ſhould not matter it; but *Polly* is tinder, and a ſpark will at once ſet her on a flame. Married! If the wench does not know her own profit, ſure ſhe knows her own pleaſure better than to make herſelf a property! My daughter to me ſhould be, like a court lady to a miniſter of ſtate, a key to the whole gang. Married! If the affair is not already done, I'll terrify her from it, by the example of our neighbours.

Mrs. *Peach.* May-hap, my dear, you may injure the girl. She loves to imitate the fine ladies, and ſhe may only allow the Captain liberties in the view of intereſt.

*Peach.* But 'tis your duty, my dear, to warn the girl againſt her ruin, and to inſtruct her how to make the moſt of her beauty. I'll go to her this moment, and ſift her. In the mean time, wife, rip out the coronets and marks of theſe dozen of cambric handkerchiefs, for I can diſpoſe of them this afternoon to a chap in the city.

---

## SCENE V.

### Mrs. *PEACHUM*.

Never was a man more out of the way in an argument than my huſband! Why muſt our *Polly*, forſooth, differ from her ſex, and love only her huſband? And why muſt *Polly*'s marriage, contrary to all obſervation, make her the leſs followed by other men? All men are thieves in love, and like a woman the better for being another's property.

AIR V. Of all the ſimple things we do, *&c.*

*A Maid is like the golden oar,*
*Which hath guineas intrinſical in't,*
*Whoſe worth is never known, before*
*It is try'd and impreſt in the mint.*

*A Wife's*

*A Wife's like a guinea in gold,*
*Stampt with the name of her spouse;*
*Now here, now there; is bought, or is sold;*
*And is current in every house.*

## SCENE VI.

### Mrs. *PEACHUM, FILCH.*

Mrs. *Peach.* Come hither, *Filch.* I am as fond of this child, as though my mind misgave me he were my own. He hath as fine a hand at picking a pocket as a woman, and is as nimble-finger'd as a juggler. If an unlucky session does not cut the rope of thy life, I pronounce, boy, thou wilt be a great man in history. Where was your post last night, my boy?

*Filch.* I ply'd at the Opera, madam; and considering 'twas neither dark nor rainy, so that there was no great hurry in getting chairs and coaches, made a tolerable hand on't. These seven handkerchiefs, madam.

Mrs. *Peach.* Colour'd ones, I see. They are of sure sale from our ware-house at *Redriff* among the sea-men.

*Filch.* And this snuff-box.

Mrs. *Peach.* Set in gold! A pretty encouragement this to a young beginner.

*Filch.* I had a fair tug at a charming gold watch. Pox take the Taylors for making the fobs so deep and narrow! It stuck by the way, and I was forc'd to make my escape under a coach. Really, madam, I fear I shall be cut off in the flower of my youth, so that every now and then (since I was pumpt) I have thoughts of taking up and going to Sea.

Mrs. *Peach.* You should go to *Hockley in the hole,* and to *Marybone,* child, to learn valour. These are the schools that have bred so many brave men. I thought, boy, by this time, thou hadst lost fear as well as shame. Poor lad! how little does he know as yet of the *Old-Baily!* For the first fact I'll ensure thee from being hang'd; and going to Sea, *Filch,* will come time enough upon a sentence of transportation. But now, since you have nothing better to do, ev'n go to your book, and learn your catechism; for really a man makes but an ill figure in the Ordinary's paper, who cannot give a satisfactory answer to his questions. But, hark you, my lad. Don't tell me a lye; for you know I hate a lyar. Do you know of any thing that hath past between captain *Macheath* and our *Polly?*

*Filch.* I beg you, Madam, don't ask me; for I must either tell a lye to you or to Miss *Polly;* for I promis'd her I would not tell.

Mrs. *Peach.* But when the honour of our family is concern'd----

*Filch.* I shall lead a sad life with Miss *Polly,* if ever she come to know that I told you. Besides, I would not willingly forfeit my own honour by betraying any body.

Mrs. *Peach.* Yonder comes my husband and *Polly.* Come, *Filch,* you shall go with me into my own room, and tell me the whole story. I'll give thee a glass of a most delicious cordial that I keep for my own drinking.

# SCENE VII.

## *PEACHUM, POLLY.*

*Polly.* I know as well as any of the fine ladies how to make the most of my self and of my man too. A woman knows how to be mercenary, though she hath never been in a court or at an assembly. We have it in our natures, papa. If I allow captain *Macheath* some trifling liberties, I have this watch and other visible marks of his favour to show for it. A girl who cannot grant some things, and refuse what is most material, will make but a poor hand of her beauty, and soon be thrown upon the common.

AIR VI.    What shall I do to show how much I love her?

*Virgins are like the fair flower in its lustre,*
    *Which in the garden enamels the ground;*
*Near it the Bees in play flutter and cluster,*
    *And gaudy Butterflies frolick around.*
*But, when once pluck'd, 'tis no longer alluring,*
    *To* Covent-Garden *'tis sent, ( as yet sweet,)*
*There fades, and shrinks, and grows past all enduring,*
    *Rots, stinks, and dies, and is trod under feet.*

*Peach.* You know, *Polly,* I am not against your toying and trifling with a customer in the way of business, or to get out a secret, or so.
But

But if I find out that you have play'd the fool and are married, you jade you, I'll cut your throat, huffy.   Now you know my mind.

## SCENE VIII.

*PEACHUM, POLLY,* Mrs. *PEACHUM.*

### AIR VII.   Oh *London* is a fine Town.

*Mrs.* Peachum, [*in a very great paffion.*]
*Our* Polly *is a fad flut! nor heeds what we have taught her.*
*I wonder any man alive will ever rear a daughter !*
*For fhe muft have both hoods and gowns, and hoops to fwell her pride,*
*With fcarfs and ftays, and gloves and lace ; and fhe will have men befide ;*
*And when fhe's dreft with care and coft, all-tempting, fine and gay,*
*As men fhould ferve a Cowcumber, fhe flings herfelf away.*

You baggage! you huffy! you inconfiderate jade! had you been hang'd, it would not have vex'd me, for that might have been your misfortune ; but to do fuch a mad thing by choice! The wench is married, husband.

*Peach.* Married! The Captain is a bold man, and will rifque any thing for money; to be fure he believes her a fortune.   Do you think your mother and I fhould have liv'd comfortably fo long together, if ever we had been married? Baggage!

*Mrs. Peach.* I knew fhe was always a proud flut; and now the wench hath play'd the fool and married, becaufe forfooth fhe would do like the Gentry.   Can you fupport the expence of a husband, huffy, in gaming, drinking and whoring? have you money enough to carry on the daily quarrels of man and wife about who fhall fquander moft? There are not many husbands and wives, who can bear the charges of plaguing one another in a handfome way.   If you muft be married, could you introduce no-body into our family but a highway-man? Why, thou foolifh jade, thou wilt be as ill us'd, and as much neglected, as if thou hadft married a Lord!

*Peach.* Let not your anger, my dear, break through the rules of decency, for the Captain looks upon himfelf in the military capacity, as a gentleman by his profeffion.   Befides what he hath already, I know

C

he

he is in a fair way of getting, or of dying ; and both thefe ways, let me tell you, are moft excellent chances for a wife. Tell me huffy, are you ruin'd or no?

Mrs. *Peach.* With *Polly*'s fortune, fhe might very well have gone off to a perfon of diftinction. Yes, that you might, you pouting flut!

*Peach.* What, is the wench dumb? Speak, or I'll make you plead by fqueezing out an anfwer from you. Are you really bound wife to him, or are you only upon liking?          [*Pinches her.*

*Polly.* Oh!                                                                [*Screaming.*

Mrs. *Peach.* How the mother is to be pitied who hath handfome daughters! Locks, bolts, bars, and lectures of morality are nothing to them : they break through them all. They have as much pleafure in cheating a father and mother, as in cheating at cards.

*Peach.* Why, *Polly*, I fhall foon know if you are married, by *Macheath*'s keeping from our houfe.

### A I R VIII.   Grim King of the Ghofts, &c.

Polly.   *Can Love be controul'd by advice?*
           *Will* Cupid *our mothers obey?*
           *Though my heart were as frozen as Ice,*
              *At his flame 'twould have melted away.*
           *When he kift me fo clofely he preft,*
              *'Twas fo fweet that I muft have comply'd:*
           *So I thought it both fafeft and beft*
              *To marry, for fear you fhould chide.*

Mrs. *Peach.* Then all the hopes of our family are gone for ever and ever!

*Peach.* And *Macheath* may hang his father and mother-in-law, in hope to get into their daughter's fortune.

*Polly.* I did not marry him (as 'tis the fafhion) cooly and delibe-rately for honour or money. But, I love him.

Mrs. *Peach.* Love him! worfe and worfe! I thought the girl had been better bred. Oh husband, husband! her folly makes me mad! my head fwims! I'm diftracted! I can't fupport myfelf---Oh! [*Faints.*

*Peach.* See, wench, to what a condition you have reduced your poor mother! a glafs of cordial, this inftant. How the poor woman takes it to heart!          [Polly *goes out, and returns with it.*

Ah, huffy, now this is the only comfort your mother has left!

                                                                        *Polly.*

*Polly.* Give her another glaſs, Sir ; my Mama drinks double the quantity whenever ſhe is out of order. This, you ſee, fetches her.

Mrs. *Peach.* The girl ſhows ſuch a readineſs, and ſo much concern, that I could almoſt find in my heart to forgive her.

AIR IX.    *O Jenny, O Jenny, where haſt thou been.*

O Polly, *you might have toy'd and kiſt.*

*By keeping men off, you keep them on.*

Polly.
   *But he ſo teaz'd me,*
   *And he ſo pleas'd me,*
*What I did, you muſt have done.*

Mrs. *Peach.* Not with a highway-man.--- You ſorry ſlut !

*Peach.* A word with you, wife. 'Tis no new thing for a wench to take man without conſent of Parents. You know 'tis the frailty of woman, my dear.

Mrs. *Peach.* Yes, indeed, the ſex is frail. But the firſt time a woman is frail, ſhe ſhould be ſomewhat nice methinks, for then or never is the time to make her fortune. After that, ſhe hath nothing to do but to guard herſelf from being found out, and ſhe may do what ſhe pleaſes.

*Peach.* Make your ſelf a little eaſy ; I have a thought ſhall ſoon ſet all matters again to rights. Why ſo melancholy, *Polly ?* ſince what is done cannot be undone, we muſt all endeavour to make the beſt of it.

Mrs. *Peach.* Well, *Polly* ; as far as one woman can forgive another, I forgive thee.---- Your father is too fond of you, huſſy.

*Polly.* Then all my ſorrows are at an end.

Mrs. *Peach.* A mighty likely ſpeech in troth, for a wench who is juſt married !

AIR X.    *Thomas, I cannot, &c.*

Polly.
*I, like a ſhip in ſtorms, was toſt ;*
*Yet afraid to put in to Land ;*
*For ſeiz'd in the port the veſſel's loſt,*
*Whoſe treaſure is contreband.*
 *The waves are laid,*
 *My duty's paid.*
*O joy beyond expreſſion !*
 *Thus, ſafe a-ſhore,*
 *I ask no more,*
*My all is in my poſſeſſion.*

C 2

*Peach.*

*Peach.* I hear cuſtomers in t'other room ; go, talk with 'em, *Polly*; but come to us again, as ſoon as they are gone.--- But, heark ye, child, if 'tis the gentleman who was here yeſterday about the repeating watch ; ſay, you believe we can't get intelligence of it, till to-morrow. For I lent it to *Suky Straddle*, to make a figure with it to-night at a tavern in *Drury-Lane*. If t'other gentleman calls for the ſilver-hilted ſword ; you know beetle-brow'd *Jemmy* hath it on, and he doth not come from *Tunbridge* till *Tueſday* night ; ſo that it cannot be had till then.

## SCENE IX.

### *PEACHUM,* Mrs. *PEACHUM.*

*Peach.* Dear wife, be a little pacified. Don't let your paſſion run away with your ſenſes. *Polly*, I grant you, hath done a raſh thing.

Mrs. *Peach.* If ſhe had had only an intrigue with the fellow, why the very beſt families have excus'd and huddled up a frailty of that ſort. 'Tis marriage, husband, that makes it a blemiſh.

*Peach.* But money, wife, is the true fuller's earth for reputations, there is not a ſpot or a ſtain but what it can take out. A rich rogue now-a-days is fit company for any gentleman ; and the world, my dear, hath not ſuch a contempt for roguery as you imagine. I tell you, wife, I can make this match turn to our advantage.

Mrs. *Peach.* I am very ſenſible, husband, that captain *Macheath* is worth money, but I am in doubt whether he hath not two or three wives already, and then if he ſhould dye in a Seſſion or two, *Polly*'s dower would come into diſpute.

*Peach.* That, indeed, is a point which ought to be conſider'd.

### AIR XI. A Soldier and a Sailor.

*A Fox may ſteal your hens, ſir,*
*A whore your health and pence, ſir,*
*Your daughter rob your cheſt, ſir,*
*Your wife may ſteal your reſt, ſir,*
 *A thief your goods and plate.*
*But this is all but picking,*
*With reſt, pence, cheſt and chicken ;*
*It ever was decreed, ſir,*
*If Lawyer's hand is fee'd, ſir,*
 *He ſteals your whole eſtate.*

The

The Lawyers are bitter enemies to those in our way. They don't care that any body should get a clandestine livelihood but themselves.

## SCENE X.

### Mrs. *PEACHUM, PEACHUM, POLLY.*

*Polly.* 'Twas only Nimming *Ned.* He brought in a damask window-curtain, a hoop-petticoat, a pair of silver candlesticks, a periwig, and one silk stocking, from the fire that happen'd last night.

*Peach.* There is not a fellow that is cleverer in his way, and saves more goods out of the fire than *Ned.* But now, *Polly*, to your affair; for matters must not be left as they are. You are married then, it seems?

*Polly.* Yes, Sir.

*Peach.* And how do you propose to live, child?

*Polly.* Like other women, Sir, upon the industry of my husband.

Mrs. *Peach.* What, is the wench turn'd fool? A highway-man's wife, like a soldier's, hath as little of his pay, as of his company.

*Peach.* And had not you the common views of a gentlewoman in your marriage, *Polly?*

*Polly.* I don't know what you mean, Sir.

*Peach.* Of a jointure, and of being a widow.

*Polly.* But I love him, Sir: how then could I have thoughts of parting with him?

*Peach.* Parting with him! Why, that is the whole scheme and intention of all Marriage-articles. The comfortable estate of widowhood, is the only hope that keeps up a wife's spirits. Where is the woman who would scruple to be a wife, if she had it in her power to be a widow whenever she pleas'd? If you have any views of this sort, *Polly*, I shall think the match not so very unreasonable.

*Polly.* How I dread to hear your advice! Yet I must beg you to explain yourself.

*Peach.* Secure what he hath got, have him peach'd the next Sessions, and then at once you are made a rich widow.

*Polly.* What, murder the man I love! The blood runs cold at my heart with the very thought of it.

*Peach.*

*Peach.* Fye, *Polly!* what hath murder to do in the affair? Since the thing sooner or later must happen, I dare say, the Captain himself would like that we should get the reward for his death sooner than a stranger. Why, *Polly,* the Captain knows, that as 'tis his employment to rob, so 'tis ours to take Robbers; every man in his business. So that there is no malice in the case.

Mrs. *Peach.* Ay, husband, now you have nick'd the matter. To have him peach'd is the only thing could ever make me forgive her.

AIR XII. Now ponder well, ye parents dear.

Polly.      *Oh, ponder well! be not severe;*
          *So save a wretched wife!*
        *For on the rope that hangs my dear*
          *Depends poor* Polly's *life.*

Mrs. *Peach.* But your duty to your parents, hussy, obliges you to hang him. What would many a wife give for such an opportunity!

*Polly.* What is a jointure, what is widow-hood to me? I know my heart. I cannot survive him.

AIR XIII. Le printemps rappelle aux armes.

     *The Turtle thus with plaintive crying,*
        *Her lover dying,*
    *The Turtle thus with plaintive crying*
        *Laments her Dove.*
     *Down she drops quite pent with sighing*
     *Pair'd in death, as pair'd in love.*

Thus, Sir, it will happen to your poor *Polly.*

Mrs. *Peach.* What, is the fool in love in earnest then? I hate thee for being particular: Why, wench, thou art a shame to thy very Sex.

*Polly.* But hear me, mother. —— If you ever lov'd ——

Mrs. *Peach.* Those cursed Play-books she reads have been her ruin. One word more, hussy, and I shall knock your brains out, if you have any.

*Peach.* Keep out of the way, *Polly,* for fear of mischief, and consider of what is propos'd to you.

Mrs. *Peach.* Away, hussy. Hang your husband, and be dutiful.

SCENE

## S C E N E  XI.

### Mrs. *PEACHUM*, *PEACHUM*.

[Polly *liſtning.*

*Mrs. Peach.* The thing, husband, muſt and ſhall be done. For the ſake of intelligence we muſt take other meaſures, and have him peach'd the next Seſſion without her conſent.  If ſhe will not know her duty, we know ours.

*Peach.* But really, my dear, it grieves one's heart to take off a great man.  When I conſider his perſonal bravery, his fine ſtratagem, how much we have already got by him, and how much more we may get, methinks I can't find in my heart to have a hand in his death.  I wiſh you could have made *Polly* undertake it.

*Mrs. Peach.* But in a caſe of neceſſity ——— our own lives are in danger.

*Peach.* Then, indeed, we muſt comply with the cuſtoms of the world, and make gratitude give way to intereſt. ——— He ſhall be taken off.

*Mrs. Peach.* I'll undertake to manage *Polly*.

*Peach.* And I'll prepare matters for the *Old-Baily*.

## S C E N E  XII.

### *POLLY.*

Now I'm a wretch, indeed. ——— Methinks I ſee him already in the cart, ſweeter and more lovely than the noſegay in his hand! ——— I hear the crowd extolling his reſolution and intrepidity! ——— What vollies of ſighs are ſent from the windows of *Holborn*, that ſo comely a youth ſhould be brought to diſgrace! —— I ſee him at the tree! the whole Circle are in tears! ——— even Butchers weep! ——— *Jack Ketch* himſelf heſitates to perform his duty, and would be glad to loſe his fee, by a reprieve.  What then will become of *Polly!* —— As yet I may inform him of their deſign, and aid him in his eſcape.   It ſhall be ſo. ——— But then he flies, abſents himſelf, and I bar myſelf from his dear dear converſation! that too will diſtract me. —— If he keep out of the way, my Papa and Mama may in time relent,

and

and we may be happy. —— If he ſtays, he is hang'd, and then he is loſt for ever! —— He intended to lye conceal'd in my room, 'till the dusk of the evening: If they are abroad I'll this inſtant let him out, leſt ſome accident ſhould prevent him.    [*Exit, and returns.*

SCENE XIII.

*POLLY, MACHEATH.*

AIR XIV.    Pretty Parrot, ſay, &c.

Mach.                *Pretty* Polly, *ſay,*
                *When I was away,*
        *Did your fancy never ſtray*
            *To ſome newer lover?*
Polly.            *Without diſguiſe,*
            *Heaving ſighs,*
            *Doating eyes,*
        *My conſtant heart diſcover.*
            *Fondly let me loll!*
Mach.        *O pretty, pretty* Poll.

*Polly.* And are *you* as fond as ever, my dear?

*Mach.* Suſpect my honour, my courage, ſuſpect any thing but my love. —— May my piſtols miſs fire, and my mare ſlip her ſhoulder while I am purſu'd, if I ever forſake thee!

*Polly.* Nay, my dear, I have no reaſon to doubt you, for I find in the Romance you lent me, none of the great Heroes were ever falſe in love.

AIR XV.    Pray, fair one, be kind.

Mach.            *My heart was ſo free,*
            *It rov'd like the Bee,*
        *'Till* Polly *my paſſion requited;*
            *I ſipt each flower,*
            *I chang'd ev'ry hour,*
        *But here ev'ry flower is united.*

*Polly.* Were you ſentenc'd to Tranſportation, ſure, my dear, you could not leave me behind you —— could you?

                                        *Mach.*

*Mach.* Is there any power, any force that could tear me from thee ? You might fooner tear a penfion out of the hands of a Courtier, a fee from a Lawyer, a pretty woman from a looking-glafs, or any woman from *Quadrille.* —— But to tear me from thee is impoffible !

### AIR XVI.   Over the hills and far away.

*Were I laid on* Greenland's *coaft,*
  *And in my arms embrac'd my lafs ;*
*Warm amidft eternal froft,*
  *Too foon the half year's night would pafs.*

Polly.  *Were I fold on* Indian *foil,*
  *Soon as the burning day was clos'd,*
*I could mock the fultry toil,*
  *When on my charmer's breaft repos'd.*

Mach.  *And I would love you all the day,*
Polly.  *Every night would kifs and play,*
Mach.  *If with me you'd fondly ftray*
Polly.  *Over the hills and far away.*

*Polly.* Yes, I would go with thee. But oh ! —— how fhall I fpeak it ? I muft be torn from thee. We muft part.

*Mach.* How ! Part !

*Polly.* We muft, we muft. —— My Papa and Mama are fet againft thy life. They now, even now are in fearch after thee. They are preparing evidence againft thee. Thy life depends upon a moment.

### AIR XVII.   Gin thou wert mine awn thing.

*O what pain it is to part !*
  *Can I leave thee, can I leave thee ?*
*O what pain it is to part !*
  *Can thy* Polly *ever leave thee ?*
*But left death my love fhould thwart,*
*And bring thee to the fatal cart,*
*Thus I tear thee from my bleeding heart !*
  *Fly hence, and let me leave thee.*

One kifs and then —— one kifs —— begone —— farewell.

D

Mach.

*Mach*. My hand, my heart, my dear, is so riveted to thine, that I cannot unloose my hold.

*Polly*. But my Papa may intercept thee, and then I should lose the very glimmering of hope.   A few weeks, perhaps, may reconcile us all.   Shall thy *Polly* hear from thee?

*Mach*. Must I then go?

*Polly*. And will not absence change your love?

*Mach*. If you doubt it, let me stay——and be hang'd.

*Polly*. O how I fear! how I tremble!—Go—but when safety will give you leave, you will be sure to see me again; for 'till then *Polly* is wretched.

### AIR XVIII.   O the broom, &c.

Mach.    *The Miser thus a shilling sees,*    [Parting, and looking back at each
   *Which he's oblig'd to pay,*    other with fondness;  he at one
  *With sighs resigns it by degrees,*    door, she at the other.
   *And fears 'tis gone for aye.*

Polly.    *The Boy thus, when his Sparrow's flown,*
   *The bird in silence eyes;*
  *But soon as out of sight 'tis gone,*
   *Whines, whimpers, sobs and cries.*

ACT

# ACT II. SCENE I.

*A Tavern near* Newgate.

Jemmy Twitcher, *Crook-finger'd* Jack, Wat Dreary, Robin *of* Bagſhot, Nimming Ned, Henry Padington, Matt *of the* Mint, Ben Budge, *and the reſt of the Gang, at the Table, with Wine, Brandy and Tobacco.*

### BEN.

UT pr'ythee, *Matt,* what is become of thy brother *Tom?* I have not ſeen him ſince my return from tranſportation.

*Matt.* Poor brother *Tom* had an accident this time twelvemonth, and ſo clever a made fellow he was, that I could not ſave him from thoſe fleaing raſcals the Surgeons; and now, poor man, he is among the Otamys at *Surgeon's-Hall.*

*Ben.* So it ſeems, his time was come.

*Jem.* But the preſent time is ours, and no body alive hath more. Why are the laws levell'd at us? are we more diſhoneſt than the reſt of mankind? what we win, gentlemen, is our own by the law of arms, and the right of conqueſt.

*Crook.* Where ſhall we find ſuch another ſet of practical philoſophers, who to a man are above the fear of Death?

*Wat.* Sound men, and true!

*Robin.* Of try'd courage, and indefatigable induſtry!

*Ned.*

*Ned.* Who is there here that would not dye for his friend?

*Harry.* Who is there here that would betray him for his interest?

*Matt.* Show me a gang of Courtiers that can say as much.

*Ben.* We are for a just partition of the world, for every man hath a right to enjoy life.

*Matt.* We retrench the superfluities of mankind. The world is avaritious, and I hate avarice. A covetous fellow, like a Jack-daw, steals what he was never made to enjoy, for the sake of hiding it. These are the robbers of mankind, for money was made for the free-hearted and generous, and where is the injury of taking from another, what he hath not the heart to make use of?

*Jem.* Our several stations for the day are fixt. Good luck attend us all. Fill the glasses.

### AIR XIX. Fill ev'ry glass, &c.

| Matt. | *Fill ev'ry glass, for wine inspires us,* |
| | *And fires us* |
| | *With courage, love and joy.* |
| | *Women and wine should life employ.* |
| | *Is there ought else on earth desirous?* |
| Chorus. | *Fill ev'ry glass, &c.* |

## SCENE II.

### To them enter MACHEATH.

*Mach.* Gentlemen, well met. My heart hath been with you this hour; but an unexpected affair hath detain'd me. No ceremony, I beg you.

*Matt.* We were just breaking up to go upon duty. Am I to have the honour of taking the air with you, Sir, this evening upon the Heath? I drink a dram now and then with the Stage-coachmen in the way of friendship and intelligence; and I know that about this time there will be passengers upon the western road, who are worth speaking with.

*Mach.* I was to have been of that party ----- but -----

*Matt.* But what, Sir?

*Mach.* Is there any man who suspects my courage?

*Matt.*

*Matt.* We have all been witneſſes of it.

*Mach.* My honour and truth to the gang?

*Matt.* I'll be anſwerable for it.

*Mach.* In the diviſion of our booty, have I ever ſhown the leaſt marks of avarice or injuſtice!

*Matt.* By theſe queſtions ſomething ſeems to have ruffled you. Are any of us ſuſpected?

*Mach.* I have a fixt confidence, gentlemen, in you all, as men of honour, and as ſuch I value and reſpect you. *Peachum* is a man that is uſeful to us.

*Matt.* Is he about to play us any foul play? I'll ſhoot him through the head.

*Mach.* I beg you, gentlemen, act with conduct and diſcretion. A piſtol is your laſt reſort.

*Matt.* He knows nothing of this meeting.

*Mach.* Buſineſs cannot go on without him. He is a man who knows the world, and is a neceſſary agent to us. We have had a ſlight difference, and till it is accommodated I ſhall be oblig'd to keep out of his way. Any private diſpute of mine ſhall be of no ill conſequence to my friends. You muſt continue to act under his direction, for the moment we break looſe from him, our gang is ruin'd.

*Matt.* As a bawd to a whore, I grant you, he is to us of great convenience.

*Mach.* Make him believe I have quitted the gang, which I can never do but with life. At our private quarters I will continue to meet you. A week or ſo will probably reconcile us.

*Matt.* Your inſtructions ſhall be obſerv'd. 'Tis now high time for us to repair to our ſeveral duties ; ſo till the evening at our quarters in *Moor-fields* we bid you farewell.

*Mach.* I ſhall wiſh my ſelf with you. Succeſs attend you.

[*Sits down melancholy at the Table.*

AIR XX.   March in *Rinaldo*, with Drums and Trumpets.

Matt.

> *Let us take the road.*
>> *Hark! I hear the ſound of coaches!*
>> *The hour of attack approaches,*
> *To your arms, brave boys, and load.*

See

*See the ball I hold!*
*Let the Chymists toil like asses,*
*Our fire their fire surpasses,*
*And turns all our lead to gold.*

[The Gang, rang'd in the front of the Stage, load their pistols, and stick them under their girdles; then go off singing the first part in Chorus.

## SCENE III.

### MACHEATH, DRAWER.

*Mach.* What a fool is a fond wench! *Polly* is most confoundedly bit.-----I love the sex. And a man who loves money, might as well be contented with one guinea, as I with one woman. The town perhaps hath been as much oblig'd to me, for recruiting it with free-hearted ladies, as to any recruiting Officer in the army. If it were not for us and the other gentlemen of the sword, *Drury-lane* would be uninhabited.

AIR XXI.    Would you have a young Virgin, &c.

*If the heart of a man is deprest with cares,*
*The mist is dispell'd when a woman appears;*
*Like the notes of a fiddle, she sweetly, sweetly*
*Raises the spirits, and charms our ears.*
　*Roses and lillies her cheeks disclose,*
　*But her ripe lips are more sweet than those.*
　　*Press her,*
　　*Caress her,*
　　*With blisses,*
　　*Her kisses*
*Dissolve us in pleasure, and soft repose.*

I must have women. There is nothing unbends the mind like them. Money is not so strong a cordial for the time.——Drawer.——
　　　　　　　　　　　　　　　　　[Enter

[*Enter Drawer.*] Is the Porter gone for all the ladies, according to my directions?

*Draw.* I expect him back every minute. But you know, Sir, you sent him as far as *Hockley in the Hole*, for three of the ladies, for one in *Vinegar Yard*, and for the rest of them somewhere about *Lewkner's Lane*. Sure some of them are below, for I hear the barr bell. As they come I will show them up.——Coming, coming.

## SCENE IV.

Macheath, *Mrs.* Coaxer, Dolly Trull, *Mrs.* Vixen, Betty Doxy, Jenny Diver, *Mrs.* Slammekin, Suky Tawdry, *and* Molly Brazen.

*Mach.* Dear Mrs. *Coaxer*, you are welcome. You look charmingly to-day. I hope you don't want the repairs of quality, and lay on paint——*Dolly Trull!* kiss me, you slut; are you as amorous as ever, hussy? You are always so taken up with stealing hearts, that you don't allow your self time to steal any thing else.——Ah *Dolly*, thou wilt ever be a Coquette!——Mrs. *Vixen*, I'm yours, I always lov'd a woman of wit and spirit; they make charming mistresses, but plaguy wives.——*Betty Doxy!* Come hither, hussy. Do you drink as hard as ever? You had better stick to good wholesome beer; for in troth, *Betty*, strong-waters will in time ruin your constitution. You should leave those to your betters.——What! and my pretty *Jenny Diver* too! As prim and demure as ever! There is not any Prude, though ever so high bred, hath a more sanctify'd look, with a more mischievous heart. Ah! thou art a dear artful hypocrite.——Mrs. *Slammekin!* as careless and genteel as ever! all you fine ladies, who know your own beauty, affect an undress——But see, here's *Suky Tawdry* come to contradict what I was saying. Every thing she gets one way she lays out upon her back. Why, *Suky*, you must keep at least a dozen Tally-men. *Molly Brazen!* [*She kisses him.*] That's well done. I love a free-hearted wench. Thou hast a most agreeable assurance, girl, and art as willing as a Turtle.——But hark! I hear musick. The Harper is at the door. *If musick be the food of Love, play on.* E'er you seat your selves, ladies, what think

you

you of a dance? Come in. [*Enter Harper*] Play the *French* Tune, that Mrs. *Slammekin* was so fond of.

> [*A Dance* a la ronde *in the* French *manner; near the end of it this Song and Chorus.*

### AIR XXII. Cotillon.

*Youth's the season made for joys,*
  *Love is then our duty;*
*She alone who that employs,*
  *Well deserves her beauty.*
   *Let's be gay,*
    *While we may,*
*Beauty's a flower despis'd in decay.*
*Youth's the season, &c.*

*Let us drink and sport to-day,*
  *Ours is not to-morrow.*
*Love with youth flies swift away,*
  *Age is nought but sorrow.*
   *Dance and sing,*
    *Time's on the wing,*
*Life never knows the return of spring.*

Chorus.  *Let us drink, &c.*

*Mach.* Now, pray ladies, take your places. Here Fellow, [*Pays the Harper.*] Bid the Drawer bring us more wine. [*Ex. Harper.*] If any of the ladies chuse gin, I hope they will be so free to call for it.

*Jenny.* You look as if you meant me. Wine is strong enough for me. Indeed, Sir, I never drink strong-waters, but when I have the Cholic.

*Mach.* Just the excuse of the fine ladies! Why, a lady of quality is never without the Cholic. I hope, Mrs. *Coaxer*, you have had good success of late in your visits among the Mercers.

*Coax.* We have so many interlopers —— Yet with industry, one may still have a little picking. I carried a silver-flower'd lutestring and a piece of black padesoy to Mr. *Peachum*'s Lock but last week.

*Vix.*

*Vix.* There's *Molly Brazen* hath the ogle of a Rattle-snake. She rivitted a Linnen-draper's eye so fast upon her, that he was nick'd of three pieces of cambric before he could look off.

*Braz.* O dear madam!——But sure nothing can come up to your handling of laces! And then you have such a sweet deluding tongue! To cheat a man is nothing; but the woman must have fine parts indeed who cheats a woman!

*Vix.* Lace, madam, lyes in a small compass, and is of easy conveyance. But you are apt, madam, to think too well of your friends.

*Coax.* If any woman hath more art than another, to be sure, 'tis *Jenny Diver*. Though her fellow be never so agreeable, she can pick his pocket as cooly, as if money were her only pleasure. Now that is a command of the passions uncommon in a woman!

*Jenny.* I never go to the tavern with a man, but in the view of business. I have other hours, and other sort of men for my pleasure. But had I your address, madam ———

*Mach.* Have done with your compliments, ladies; and drink about: You are not so fond of me, *Jenny*, as you use to be.

*Jenny.* 'Tis not convenient, Sir, to show my fondness among so many rivals. 'Tis your own choice, and not the warmth of my inclination, that will determine you.

### A I R  XXIII.　All in a misty morning.

*Before the barn-door crowing,*
　*The Cock by Hens attended,*
*His eyes around him throwing,*
　*Stands for a while suspended.*
*Then one he singles from the crew,*
　*And cheers the happy Hen;*
*With how do you do, and how do you do,*
　*And how do you do again.*

*Mach.* Ah *Jenny!* thou art a dear slut.

*Trull.* Pray, madam, were you ever in keeping?

*Tawd.* I hope, madam, I ha'nt been so long upon the town, but I have met with some good fortune as well as my neighbours.

*Trull.* Pardon me, madam, I meant no harm by the question; 'twas only in the way of conversation.

E

*Tawd.*

*Tawd.* Indeed, madam, if I had not been a fool, I might have liv'd very handsomely with my last friend. But upon his missing five guineas, he turn'd me off. Now I never suspected he had counted them.

*Slam.* Who do you look upon, madam, as your best sort of keepers?

*Trull.* That, madam, is thereafter as they be.

*Slam.* I, madam, was once kept by a *Jew*; and bating their religion, to women they are a good sort of people.

*Tawd.* Now for my part, I own I like an old fellow: for we always make them pay for what they can't do.

*Vix.* A spruce Prentice, let me tell you, ladies, is no ill thing, they bleed freely. I have sent at least two or three dozen of them in my time to the Plantations.

*Jen.* But to be sure, Sir, with so much good fortune as you have had upon the road, you must be grown immensely rich.

*Mach.* The road, indeed, hath done me justice, but the gaming-table hath been my ruin.

AIR XXIV.    When once I lay with another man's wife.

Jen. *The Gamesters and Lawyers are jugglers alike,*
 *If they meddle your all is in danger :*
 *Like Gypsies, if once they can finger a souse,*
 *Your pockets they pick, and they pilfer your house,*
 *And give your estate to a stranger.*

A man of courage should never put any thing to the risque, but his life. These are the tools of a man of honour. Cards and Dice are only fit for cowardly cheats, who prey upon their friends.

    [*She takes up his Pistol.* Tawdry *takes up the other.*

*Tawd.* This, Sir, is fitter for your hand. Besides your loss of money, 'tis a loss to the ladies. Gaming takes you off from women. How fond could I be of you! but before company, 'tis ill bred.

*Mach.* Wanton hussies!

*Jen.* I must and will have a kiss to give my wine a zest.

  [*They take him about the neck, and make signs to* Peachum *and Constables, who rush in upon him.*

SCENE

## SCENE V.

*To them P E A C H U M and Constables.*

*Peach.* I seize you, Sir, as my prisoner.

*Mach.* Was this well done, *Jenny?* —— Women are decoy Ducks; who can trust them! Beasts, Jades, Jilts, Harpies, Furies, Whores!

*Peach.* Your case, Mr. *Macheath*, is not particular. The greatest Heroes have been ruin'd by women. But, to do them justice, I must own they are a pretty sort of creatures, if we could trust them. You must now, Sir, take your leave of the ladies, and if they have a mind to make you a visit, they will be sure to find you at home. The gentleman, ladies, lodges in *Newgate*. Constables, wait upon the Captain to his lodgings.

### AIR XXV.   When first I laid siege to my *Chloris*.

Mach.   *At the Tree I shall suffer with pleasure,*

   *At the Tree I shall suffer with pleasure,*

   *Let me go where I will,*

   *In all kinds of ill,*

   *I shall find no such Furies as these are.*

*Peach.* Ladies, I'll take care the reckoning shall be discharg'd.

[*Ex.* Macheath, *guarded with* Peachum *and Constables.*

## SCENE VI.

*The Women remain.*

*Vix.* Look ye, Mrs. *Jenny,* though Mr. *Peachum* may have made a private bargain with you and *Suky Tawdry* for betraying the Captain, as we were all assisting, we ought all to share alike.

*Coax.* I think Mr. *Peachum*, after so long an acquaintance, might have trusted me as well as *Jenny Diver.*

*Slam.* I am sure at least three men of his hanging, and in a year's time too, (if he did me justice) should be set down to my account.

*Trull.* Mrs. *Slammekin,* that is not fair. For you know one of them was taken in bed with me.   E 2   *Jenny.*

*Jenny.* As far as a bowl of punch or a treat, I believe Mrs. *Suky* will join with me. ———— As for any thing elfe, ladies, you cannot in confcience expect it.

*Slam.* Dear madam ———

*Trull.* I would not for the world ———

*Slam.* 'Tis impoffible for me ———

*Trull.* As I hope to be fav'd, madam ———

*Slam.* Nay, then I muft ftay here all night ———

*Trull.* Since you command me.    [*Exeunt with great Ceremony.*

## SCENE VII.    *Newgate.*

### LOCKIT, Turnkeys, MACHEATH, Conftables.

*Luc.* Noble Captain, you are welcome. You have not been a lodger of mine this year and half. You know the cuftom, Sir. Garnifh, Captain, garnifh. Hand me down thofe fetters there.

*Mach.* Thofe, Mr. *Lockit*, feem to be the heavieft of the whole fet. With your leave, I fhould like the further pair better.

*Lock.* Look ye, Captain, we know what is fitteft for our prifoners. When a gentleman ufes me with civility, I always do the beft I can to pleafe him ——— Hand them down I fay ——— We have them of all prices, from one guinea to ten, and 'tis fitting every gentleman fhould pleafe himfelf.

*Mach.* I underftand you, Sir. [*Gives money.*] The fees here are fo many, and fo exorbitant, that few fortunes can bear the expence of getting off handfomly, or of dying like a gentleman.

*Lock.* Thofe, I fee, will fit the Captain better. ——— Take down the further pair. Do but examine them, Sir ——— Never was better work. —— How genteely they are made! —— They will fit as eafy as a glove, and the niceft man in *England* might not be afham'd to wear them. [*He puts on the chains.*] If I had the beft gentleman in the land in my cuftody I could not equip him more handfomly. And fo, Sir —— I now leave you to your private meditations.

SCENE

## SCENE VIII.

### *M A C H E A T H.*

**A I R  XXVI.**  Courtiers, Courtiers think it no harm.

*Man may escape from rope and gun;*
  *Nay, some have out-liv'd the Doctor's pill :*
*Who takes a woman must be undone,*
  *That Basilisk is sure to kill.*
*The Fly that sips treacle is lost in the sweets,*
*So he that tastes woman, woman, woman,*
  *He that tastes woman, ruin meets.*

To what a woful plight have I brought my self! Here must I (all day long, 'till I am hang'd) be confin'd to hear the reproaches of a wench who lays her ruin at my door. ------ I am in the custody of her father, and to be sure if he knows of the matter, I shall have a fine time on't betwixt this and my execution. ---- But I promis'd the wench marriage. ---- What signifies a promise to a woman ? does not man in marriage itself promise a hundred things that he never means to perform ? Do all we can, women will believe us ; for they look upon a promise as an excuse for following their own inclinations. ---- But here comes *Lucy*, and I cannot get from her ---- wou'd I were deaf !

## SCENE IX.

### *M A C H E A T H, L U C Y.*

*Lucy.* You base man you, ---- how can you look me in the face after what hath past between us ? ---- See here, perfidious wretch, how I am forc'd to bear about the load of Infamy you have laid upon me ---- O *Macheath* ! thou hast robb'd me of my quiet ---- to see thee tortur'd would give me pleasure.

**A I R.**

### AIR XXVII.   A lovely Lass to a Friar came.

*Thus when a good hufwife fees a Rat*
*In her trap in the morning taken,*
*With pleafure her heart goes pit a pat,*
*In revenge for her lofs of bacon.*
*Then fhe throws him*
*To the Dog or Cat,*
*To be worried, crufh'd and fhaken.*

*Mach.* Have you no bowels, no tendernefs, my dear *Lucy*, to fee a husband in thefe circumftances?

*Lucy.* A husband!

*Mach.* In ev'ry refpect but the form, and that, my dear, may be faid over us at any time.---Friends fhould not infift upon ceremonies. From a man of honour, his word is as good as his bond.

*Lucy.* 'Tis the pleafure of all you fine men to infult the women you have ruin'd.

### AIR XXVIII..   'Twas when the Sea was roaring.

*How cruel are the traytors,*
*Who lye and fwear in jeft,*
*To cheat unguarded creatures*
*Of virtue, fame, and reft !*
*Whoever fteals a fhilling,*
*Thro' fhame the guilt conceals :*
*In love the perjur'd villain*
*With boafts the theft reveals.*

*Mach.* The very firft opportunity, my dear, *(*have but patience*)* you fhall be my wife in whatever manner you pleafe.

*Lucy.* Infinuating monfter! And fo you think I know nothing of the affair of Mifs *Polly Peachum*.---- I could tear thy eyes out !

*Mach.* Sure *Lucy*, you can't be fuch a fool as to be jealous of *Polly* !

*Lucy.* Are you not married to her, you brute, you?

*Mach.* Married! Very good. The wench gives it out only to vex thee, and to ruin me in thy good opinion. 'Tis true, I go to the

house;

houfe; I chat with the girl, I kifs her, I fay a thoufand things to her (as all gentlemen do) that mean nothing, to divert my felf; and now the filly jade hath fet it about that I am married to her, to let me know what fhe would be at. Indeed, my dear *Lucy*, thefe violent paffions may be of ill confequence to a woman in your condition.

*Lucy.* Come, come, Captain, for all your affurance, you know that Mifs *Polly* hath put it out of your power to do me the juftice you promis'd me.

*Mach.* A jealous woman believes ev'ry thing her paffion fuggefts. To convince you of my fincerity, if we can find the Ordinary, I fhall have no fcruples of making you my wife; and I know the confequence of having two at a time.

*Lucy.* That you are only to be hang'd, and fo get rid of them both.

*Mach.* I am ready, my dear *Lucy*, to give you fatisfaction ---- if you think there is any in marriage. ----- What can a man of honour fay more?

*Lucy.* So then it feems, you are not married to Mifs *Polly*.

*Mach.* You know, *Lucy*, the girl is prodigioufly conceited. No man can fay a civil thing to her, but (like other fine ladies) her vanity makes her think he's her own for ever and ever.

### AIR XXIX.    The Sun had loos'd his weary teams.

*The firft time at the looking-glafs*
 *The mother fets her daughter,*
*The Image ftrikes the fmiling lafs*
 *With felf-love ever after.*
*Each time fhe looks, fhe, fonder grown,*
 *Thinks ev'ry charm grows ftronger:*
*But alas, vain maid, all eyes but your own*
 *Can fee you are not younger.*

When women confider their own beauties, they are all alike unreafonable in their demands; for they expect their lovers fhould like them as long as they like themfelves.

*Lucy.* Yonder is my father ---- perhaps this way we may light upon the Ordinary, who fhall try if you will be as good as your word. ---- For I long to be made an honeft woman.

SCENE

## SCENE X.

*PEACHUM, LOCKIT with an Account-Book.*

*Lock.* In this laſt affair, brother *Peachum*, we are agreed. You have conſented to go halves in *Macheath*.

*Peach.* We ſhall never fall out about an execution. ---- But as to that article, pray how ſtands our laſt year's account?

*Lock.* If you will run your eye over it, you'll find 'tis fair and clearly ſtated.

*Peach.* This long arrear of the government is very hard upon us! Can it be expected that we ſhould hang our acquaintance for nothing, when our betters will hardly ſave theirs without being paid for it. Unleſs the people in employment pay better, I promiſe them for the future, I ſhall let other rogues live beſides their own.

*Lock.* Perhaps, brother, they are afraid theſe matters may be carried too far. We are treated too by them with contempt, as if our profeſſion were not reputable.

*Peach.* In one reſpect indeed, our employment may be reckon'd diſhoneſt, becauſe, like great Stateſmen, we encourage thoſe who betray their friends.

*Lock.* Such language, brother, any where elſe, might turn to your prejudice. Learn to be more guarded, I beg you.

AIR XXX. How happy are we, &c.

*When you cenſure the age,*
*Be cautious and ſage,*
*Leſt the Courtiers offended ſhould be :*
*If you mention vice or bribe,*
*'Tis ſo pat to all the tribe;*
*Each cries —— That was levell'd at me.*

*Peach.* Here's poor *Ned Clincher*'s name, I ſee. Sure, brother *Lockit*, there was a little unfair proceeding in *Ned*'s caſe: for he told me in the condemn'd hold, that for value receiv'd, you had promis'd him a Seſſion or two longer without moleſtation.

*Lock.* Mr. *Peachum*, ---- this is the firſt time my honour was ever call'd in queſtion.

*Peach.*

*Peach.* Bufinefs is at an end---if once we act difhonourably.

*Lock.* Who accufes me?

*Peach.* You are warm, brother.

*Lock.* He that attacks my honour, attacks my livelyhood.---- And this ufage ---- Sir ---- is not to be born.

*Peach.* Since you provoke me to fpeak ---- I muft tell you too, that Mrs. *Coaxer* charges you with defrauding her of her information-money, for the apprehending of curl-pated *Hugh.* Indeed, indeed, brother, we muft punctually pay our Spies, or we fhall have no Information.

*Lock.* Is this language to me, Sirrah ---- who have fav'd you from the gallows, Sirrah !                                *[Collaring each other.*

*Peach.* If I am hang'd, it fhall be for ridding the world of an arrant rafcal.

*Lock.* This hand fhall do the office of the halter you deferve, and throttle you ---- you dog !----

*Peach.* Brother, brother, ----- we are both in the wrong ---- we fhall be both lofers in the difpute ---- for you know we have it in our power to hang each other.  You fhould not be fo paffionate.

*Lock.* Nor you fo provoking.

*Peach.* 'Tis our mutual intereft; 'tis for the intereft of the world we fhould agree.  If I faid any thing, brother, to the prejudice of your character, I ask pardon.

*Lock.* Brother *Peachum* ----- I can forgive as well as refent. ———— Give me your hand.  Sufpicion does not become a friend.

*Peach.* I only meant to give you occafion to juftifie yourfelf: But I muft now ftep home, for I expect the gentleman about this Snuff-box, that *Filch* nimm'd two nights ago in the Park.  I appointed him at this hour.

## SCENE XI.
### LOCKIT, LUCY.

*Lock.* Whence come you, huffy?

*Lucy.* My tears might anfwer that queftion.

*Lock.* You have then been whimpering and fondling, like a Spaniel, over the fellow that hath abus'd you.

*Lucy.* One can't help love; one can't cure it.  'Tis not in my power to obey you, and hate him.

F

*Lock.* Learn to bear your husband's death like a reasonable woman. 'Tis not the fashion, now-a-days, so much as to affect sorrow up-on these occasions.   No woman would ever marry, if she had not the chance of mortality for a release.   Act like a woman of spirit, hussy, and thank your father for what he is doing.

### A I R  XXXI.   Of a noble Race was *Shenkin.*

Polly.         *Is then his fate decreed, Sir ?*
                *Such a man can I think of quitting ?*
        *When first we met, so moves me yet,*
            *O see how my heart is splitting !*

*Lock.* Look ye, *Lucy* ---- there is no saving him. ---- So,  I think, you must ev'n do like other widows ---- buy your self weeds, and be cheerful.

### A I R  XXXII.

*You'll think, e'er many days ensue,*
    *This sentence not severe ;*
*I hang your husband, child, 'tis true,*
    *But with him hang your care.*
        *Twang dang dillo dee.*

Like a good wife, go moan over your dying husband.   That, child, is your duty ---- consider, girl, you can't have the man and the money too ---- so make yourself as easy as you can by getting all you can from him.

---

### S C E N E   XII.

#### *L U C Y,  M A C H E A T H.*

*Lucy.* Though the Ordinary was out of the way to-day, I hope, my dear, you will, upon the first opportunity, quiet my scruples—— Oh Sir ! —— my father's hard heart is not to be soften'd, and I am in the utmost despair.

*Mach.* But if I could raise a small sum —— would not twenty Gui-neas, think you, move him ? —— Of all the arguments in the way
                                                                    of

of bufinefs, the perquifite is the moft prevailing. —— Your father's perquifites for the efcape of prifoners muft amount to a confiderable fum in the year.    Money well tim'd, and properly apply'd, will do any thing.

### A I R  XXXIII.    *London* Ladies.

*If you at an Office folicit your due,*
*    And would not have matters neglected;*
*You muft quicken the Clerk with the perquifite too,*
*    To do what his duty directed.*
*Or would you the frowns of a lady prevent,*
*    She too has this palpable failing,*
*The perquifite foftens her into confent;*
*    That reafon with all is prevailing.*

*Lucy.* What love or money can do fhall be done: for all my comfort depends upon your fafety.

## S C E N E  XIII.

### *LUCY, MACHEATH, POLLY.*

*Polly.* Where is my dear husband? ---- Was a rope ever intended for this neck! --- O let me throw my arms about it, and throttle thee with love! --- Why doft thou turn away from me? --- 'Tis thy *Polly* --- 'tis thy wife.

*Mach.* Was ever fuch an unfortunate rafcal as I am!

*Lucy.* Was there ever fuch another villain!

*Polly.* O *Macheath!* was it for this we parted? Taken! Imprifon'd! Try'd! Hang'd! ---- cruel reflection! I'll ftay with thee 'till death ---- no force fhall tear thy dear wife from thee now. —— What means my love? —— Not one kind word! not one kind look! think what thy *Polly* fuffers to fee thee in this condition.

### A I R  XXXIV.    All in the Downs, &c.

*Thus when the Swallow, feeking prey,*
*    Within the fafh is clofely pent,*
*His confort with bemoaning lay,*
*    Without fits pining for th' event.*

F 2

*Her*

*Her chatt'ring lovers all around her skim ;*
*She heeds them not (poor bird) her soul's with him.*

*Mach.* I must disown her. [*Aside.*] The wench is distracted.

*Lucy.* Am I then bilk'd of my virtue? Can I have no reparation? Sure men were born to lye, and women to believe them! O Villain! Villain!

*Polly.* Am I not thy wife?——Thy neglect of me, thy aversion to me too severely proves it.——Look on me.——Tell me, am I not thy wife?

*Lucy.* Perfidious wretch!

*Polly.* Barbarous husband!

*Lucy.* Hadst thou been hang'd five months ago, I had been happy.

*Polly.* And I too———If you had been kind to me 'till death, it would not have vex'd me———And that's no very unreasonable request, (though from a wife) to a man who hath not above seven or eight days to live.

*Lucy.* Art thou then married to another? Hast thou two wives, monster?

*Mach.* If women's tongues can cease for an answer——hear me.

*Lucy.* I won't.——Flesh and blood can't bear my usage.

*Polly.* Shall I not claim my own? Justice bids me speak.

AIR XXXV.   Have you heard of a frolicksome ditty.

Mach.      *How happy could I be with either,*
              *Were t'other dear charmer away!*
           *But while you thus teaze me together,*
              *To neither a word will I say ;*
                 *But tol de rol, &c.*

*Polly.* Sure, my dear, there ought to be some preference shown to a wife! At least she may claim the appearance of it. He must be distracted with his misfortunes, or he cou'd not use me thus!

*Lucy.* O Villain, Villain! thou hast deceiv'd me———I could even inform against thee with pleasure. Not a Prude wishes more heartily to have facts against her intimate acquaintance, than I now wish to have facts against thee. I would have her satisfaction, and they should all out.

AIR

### AIR XXXVI. Irish Trot.

Polly. *I'm bubbled.*

Lucy. *- - - - - - - I'm bubbled.*

Polly. *Oh how I am troubled!*

Lucy. *Bambouzled, and bit!*

Polly. *- - - - - - - - - - - My distresses are doubled.*

Lucy. *When you come to the Tree, should the Hangman refuse,*
*These fingers, with pleasure, could fasten the noose.*

Polly. *I'm bubbled, &c.*

*Mach.* Be pacified, my dear *Lucy* ---- This is all a fetch of *Polly*'s to make me desperate with you in case I get off. If I am hang'd, she would fain have the credit of being thought my widow ----- Really, *Polly*, this is no time for a dispute of this sort; for whenever you are talking of marriage, I am thinking of hanging.

*Polly.* And hast thou the heart to persist in disowning me?

*Mach.* And hast thou the heart to persist in persuading me that I am married? Why, *Polly*, dost thou seek to aggravate my misfortunes?

*Lucy.* Really, Miss *Peachum*, you but expose yourself. Besides, 'tis barbarous in you to worry a gentleman in his circumstances.

### AIR XXXVII.

Polly.  *Cease your funning;*
*Force or cunning*
*Never shall my heart trapan.*
*All these sallies*
*Are but malice*
*To seduce my constant man.*
*'Tis most certain,*
*By their flirting*
*Women oft have envy shown:*
*Pleas'd, to ruin*
*Others wooing;*
*Never happy in their own!*

*Polly.*

*Polly.* Decency, madam, methinks might teach you to behave yourself with some reserve with the husband, while his wife is present.

*Mach.* But seriously, *Polly*, this is carrying the joke a little too far.

*Lucy.* If you are determin'd, madam, to raise a disturbance in the prison, I shall be oblig'd to send for the Turnkey to shew you the door. I am sorry, madam, you force me to be so ill-bred.

*Polly.* Give me leave to tell you, madam; these forward Airs don't become you in the least, madam. And my duty, madam, obliges me to stay with my husband, madam.

AIR XXXVIII.  Good-morrow, Gossip Joan.

Lucy.        *Why how now, madam* Flirt?
                *If you thus must chatter,*
            *And are for flinging dirt,*
                *Let's try who best can spatter;*
                    *Madam* Flirt!

Polly.        *Why how now, saucy Jade;*
                *Sure the wench is tipsy!*
            *How can you see me made*                    [To him.
                *The scoff of such a Gipsy?*
                    *Saucy Jade!*                        [To her.

SCENE XIV.

*LUCY, MACHEATH, POLLY, PEACHUM.*

*Peach.* Where's my wench? Ah hussy! hussy! ———Come you home, you slut; and when your fellow is hang'd, hang yourself, to make your family some amends.

*Polly.* Dear, dear father, do not tear me from him ———I must speak; I have more to say to him——Oh! twist thy fetters about me, that he may not haul me from thee!

*Peach.* Sure all women are alike! If ever they commit the folly, they are sure to commit another by exposing themselves —— Away —— Not a word more ——You are my prisoner now, hussy.

AIR

AIR XXXIX. Irish Howl.

**Polly.**   *No power on earth can e'er divide*
*The knot that sacred Love hath ty'd.*
*When parents draw against our mind,*
*The true-love's knot they faster bind.*
*Oh, oh ray, oh Amborah ——— oh, oh, &c.*

[Holding *Macheath*, *Peachum* pulling her.

## SCENE XV.

### *LUCY, MACHEATH.*

*Mach.* I am naturally compassionate, wife; so that I could not use the wench as she deserv'd; which made you at first suspect there was something in what she said.

*Lucy.* Indeed, my dear, I was strangely puzzled.

*Mach.* If that had been the case, her father would never have brought me into this circumstance —— No, *Lucy*, —— I had rather dye than be false to thee.

*Lucy.* How happy am I, if you say this from your heart! For I love thee so, that I could sooner bear to see thee hang'd than in the arms of another.

*Mach.* But couldst thou bear to see me hang'd?

*Lucy.* O *Macheath*, I can never live to see that day.

*Mach.* You see, *Lucy*, in the account of Love you are in my debt; and you must now be convinc'd, that I rather chuse to die than be another's. —— Make me, if possible, love thee more, and let me owe my life to thee —— If you refuse to assist me, *Peachum* and your father will immediately put me beyond all means of escape.

*Lucy.* My father, I know, hath been drinking hard with the Prisoners: and I fancy he is now taking his nap in his own room ——— If I can procure the keys, shall I go off with thee, my dear?

*Mach.* If we are together, 'twill be impossible to lye conceal'd. As soon as the search begins to be a little cool, I will send to thee —— 'Till then my heart is thy prisoner.

*Lucy,*

*Lucy.* Come then, my dear husband——owe thy life to me——
and though you love me not——be grateful——But that *Polly* runs
in my head ſtrangely.

*Mach.* A moment of time may make us unhappy for-ever.

AIR XL.   The Laſs of *Patie*'s Mill.

Lucy.

> *I like the Fox ſhall grieve,*
>> *Whoſe mate hath left her ſide,*
> *Whom Hounds, from morn to eve,*
>> *Chaſe o'er the country wide.*
> *Where can my lover hide?*
>> *Where cheat the wary pack?*
> *If Love be not his guide,*
>> *He never will come back!*

ACT

# ACT III. SCENE I.

## SCENE *Newgate.*

### *L O C K I T, L U C Y.*

#### LOCKIT.

O be fure, wench, you muſt have been aiding and abetting to help him to this eſcape.

*Lucy.* Sir, here hath been *Peachum* and his daughter *Polly*, and to be fure they know the ways of *Newgate* as well as if they had been born and bred in the place all their lives. Why muſt all your ſuſpicion light upon me?

*Lock.* Lucy, *Lucy*, I will have none of theſe ſhuffling anſwers.

*Lucy.* Well then —— If I know any thing of him I wiſh I may be burnt!

*Lock.* Keep your temper, *Lucy*, or I ſhall pronounce you guilty.

*Lucy.* Keep yours, Sir, —— I do wiſh I may be burnt. I do —— And what can I ſay more to convince you?

*Lock.* Did he tip handſomely? —— How much did he come down with? Come huſſy, don't cheat your father; and I ſhall not be angry with you —— Perhaps, you have made a better bargain with him than I could have done — How much, my good girl?

*Lucy.* You know, Sir, I am fond of him, and would have given money to have kept him with me.

*Lock.* Ah *Lucy!* thy education might have put thee more upon thy guard; for a girl in the bar of an Ale-houſe is always beſieg'd.

*Lucy.* Dear Sir, mention not my education —— for 'twas to that I owe my ruin.

G

A I R

AIR XLI.   *If Love's a sweet passion, &c.*

*When young at the bar you first taught me to score,*
*And bid me be free of my lips, and no more;*
*I was kiss'd by the Parson, the Squire, and the Sot:*
*When the guest was departed, the kiss was forgot.*
*But his kiss was so sweet, and so closely he prest,*
*That I languish'd and pin'd 'till I granted the rest.*

If you can forgive me, Sir, I will make a fair confession, for to be sure he hath been a most barbarous villain to me.

*Lock.* And so you have let him escape, hussy——have you?

*Lucy.* When a woman loves; a kind look, a tender word can persuade her to any thing——and I could ask no other bribe.

*Lock.* Thou wilt always be a vulgar slut, *Lucy*——If you would not be look'd upon as a fool, you should never do any thing but upon the foot of interest.  Those that act otherwise are their own bubbles.

*Lucy.* But Love, Sir, is a misfortune that may happen to the most discreet woman, and in love we are all fools alike.——Notwithstanding all he swore, I am now fully convinc'd that *Polly Peachum* is actually his wife.——Did I let him escape, (fool that I was!) to go to her?——*Polly* will wheedle her self into his money, and then *Peachum* will hang him, and cheat us both.

*Lock.* So I am to be ruin'd, because, forsooth, you must be in love!——a very pretty excuse!

*Lucy.* I could murder that impudent happy strumpet:——I gave him his life, and that creature enjoys the sweets of it.——Ungrateful *Macheath!*

AIR XLII.   *South-Sea Ballad.*

*My love is all madness and folly,*
*  Alone I lye,*
*   Toss, tumble, and cry,*
*What a happy creature is* Polly!
*Was e'er such a wretch as I!*
*With rage I redden like scarlet,*
*That my dear inconstant Varlet,*

*Stark blind to my charms,*
*Is loft in the arms*
*Of that Jilt, that inveigling Harlot!*
*Stark blind to my charms,*
*Is loft in the arms*
*Of that Jilt, that inveigling Harlot!*
*This, this my refentment alarms.*

*Lock.* And fo, after all this mifchief, I muft ftay here to be enter-tain'd with your catterwauling, miftrefs Pufs!—— Out of my fight, wanton Strumpet! you fhall faft and mortify yourfelf into reafon, with now and then a little handfome difcipline to bring you to your fenfes.——Go.

## SCENE II.

### L O C K I T.

*Peachum* then intends to outwit me in this affair; but I'll be even with him.—— The dog is leaky in his liquor, fo I'll ply him that way, get the fecret from him, and turn this affair to my own advantage.—— Lions, Wolves, and Vulturs don't live together in herds, droves or flocks.———Of all animals of prey, man is the only fociable one. Every one of us preys upon his neighbour, and yet we herd toge-ther.——*Peachum* is my companion, my friend—According to the cuftom of the world, indeed, he may quote thoufands of Precedents for cheating me———And fhall not I make ufe of the privilege of friendfhip to make him a return?

### AIR XLIII.   *Packington*'s Pound.

*Thus Gamefters united in friendfhip are found,*
*Though they know that their induftry all is a cheat;*
*They flock to their prey at the Dice-box's found,*
*And join to promote one another's deceit.*
     *But if by mifhap*
     *They fail of a chap,*
*To keep in their hands, they each other entrap.*
*Like Pikes, lank with hunger, who mifs of their ends,*
*They bite their companions, and prey on their friends.*

Now,

Now, *Peachum*, you and I, like honeft Tradefmen, are to have a fair tryal which of us two can over-reach the other.——*Lucy.*—— [*Enter* Lucy.] Are there any of *Peachum*'s people now in the houfe?

*Lucy.* Filch, Sir, is drinking a quartern of Strong-waters in the next room with black *Moll.*

*Lock.* Bid him come to me.

---

## SCENE III.

### LOCKIT, FILCH.

*Lock.* Why, boy, thou lookeft as if thou wert half ftarv'd; like a fhotten Herring.

*Filch.* One had need have the conftitution of a horfe to go thorough the bufinefs.——Since the favourite Child-getter was difabled by a mis-hap, I have pick'd up a little money by helping the ladies to a pregnancy againft their being call'd down to fentence.—— But if a man cannot get an honeft livelihood any eafier way, I am fure, 'tis what I can't undertake for another Seffion.

*Lock.* Truly, if that great man fhould tip off, 'twould be an irreparable lofs. The vigor and prowefs of a Knight-errant never fav'd half the ladies in diftrefs that he hath done.—— But, boy, can'ft thou tell me where thy mafter is to be found?

*Filch.* At his * Lock, Sir, at the *Crooked Billet.*

*Lock.* Very well.—— I have nothing more with you. [*Ex.* Filch. I'll go to him there, for I have many important affairs to fettle with him; and in the way of thofe tranfactions, I'll artfully get into his fecret.—— So that *Macheath* fhall not remain a day longer out of my clutches.

---

## SCENE IV. *A Gaming-Houfe.*

### MACHEATH *in a fine tarnifh'd Coat,* BEN BUDGE, MATT *of the Mint.*

*Mach.* I am forry, gentlemen, the road was fo barren of money. When my friends are in difficulties, I am always glad that my fortune can be ferviceable to them. [*Gives them money.*] You fee, gentlemen, I am not a meer Court friend, who profeffes every thing and will do nothing.                                    A I R

* A Cant word, fignifying, a Warehoufe where ftolen goods are depofited.

### AIR XLIV. Lillibulero.

*The modes of the Court so common are grown,*
*That a true friend can hardly be met;*
*Friendship for interest is but a loan,*
*Which they let out for what they can get.*
*'Tis true, you find*
*Some friends so kind,*
*Who will give you good counsel themselves to defend.*
*In sorrowful ditty,*
*They promise, they pity,*
*But shift you for money, from friend to friend.*

But we, gentlemen, have still honour enough to break through the corruptions of the world. —— And while I can serve you, you may command me.

*Ben.* It grieves my heart that so generous a man should be involv'd in such difficulties, as oblige him to live with such ill company, and herd with gamesters.

*Matt.* See the partiality of mankind! —— One man may steal a horse, better than another look over a hedge. —— Of all mechanics, of all servile handycrafts-men, a gamester is the vilest. But yet, as many of the Quality are of the profession, he is admitted amongst the politest company. I wonder we are not more respected.

*Mach.* There will be deep play to-night at *Marybone,* and consequently money may be pick'd up upon the road. Meet me there, and I'll give you the hint who is worth setting.

*Matt.* The fellow with a brown coat with a narrow gold binding, I am told, is never without money.

*Mach.* What do you mean, *Matt?* —— Sure you will not think of meddling with him! —— He's a good honest kind of a fellow, and one of us.

*Ben.* To be sure, Sir, we will put our selves under your direction.

*Mach.* Have an eye upon the money-lenders. —— A *Rouleau,* or two, would prove a pretty sort of an expedition. I hate extortion.

*Matt.* Those *Rouleaus* are very pretty things. —— I hate your Bank bills —— there is such a hazard in putting them off.

*Mach.*

*Mach.* There is a certain man of diſtinction, who in his time hath nick'd me out of a great deal of the ready.  He is in my caſh, *Ben* ; —I'll point him out to you this evening, and you ſhall draw upon him for the debt. ———— The company are met ; I hear the Dice-box in the other room.  So, gentlemen, your ſervant.  You'll meet me at *Marybone*.

## SCENE V. *Peachum's Lock.*

### *A Table with Wine, Brandy, Pipes and Tobacco.*

#### PEACHUM, LOCKIT.

*Lock.* The Coronation account, brother *Peachum*, is of ſo intricate a nature, that I believe it will never be ſettled.

*Peach.* It conſiſts indeed of a great variety of articles. —— It was worth to our people, in fees of different kinds, above ten inſtalments. —— This is part of the account, brother, that lies open before us.

*Lock.* A lady's tail of rich Brocade —— that, I ſee, is diſpos'd of.

*Peach.* To Mrs. *Diana Trapes*, the Tally-woman, and ſhe will make a good hand on't in ſhoes and ſlippers, to trick out young ladies, upon their going into keeping. ————

*Lock.* But I don't ſee any article of the Jewels.

*Peach.* Thoſe are ſo well known, that they muſt be ſent abroad —— you'll find them enter'd under the article of Exportation. —— As for the Snuff-boxes, Watches, Swords, &c. —— I thought it beſt to enter them under their ſeveral heads.

*Lock.* Seven and twenty women's pockets compleat ; with the ſeveral things therein contain'd ; all ſeal'd, number'd, and enter'd.

*Peach.* But, brother, it is impoſſible for us now to enter upon this affair. —— We ſhould have the whole day before us. —— Beſides, the account of the laſt half year's Plate is in a book by it ſelf, which lies at the other Office.

*Lock.* Bring us then more liquor. —— To-day ſhall be for pleaſure —— to-morrow for buſineſs. —— Ah brother, thoſe daughters of ours are two ſlippery huſſies — keep a watchful eye upon *Polly*, and *Macheath* in a day or two ſhall be our own again.

AIR

AIR XLV.  Down in the North Country.

Lock.  *What Gudgeons are we men!*
*Ev'ry woman's eafy prey.*
*Though we have felt the hook, agen*
*We bite, and they betray.*

*The bird that hath been trapt,*
*When he hears his calling mate,*
*To her he flies, again he's clapt*
*Within the wiry grate.*

*Peach.* But what fignifies catching the Bird, if your daughter *Lucy* will fet open the door of the Cage?

*Lock.* If men were anfwerable for the follies and frailties of their wives and daughters, no friends could keep a good correfpondence together for two days.——This is unkind of you, brother ; for among good friends, what they fay or do goes for nothing.

*Enter a Servant.*

*Serv.* Sir, here's Mrs. *Diana Trapes* wants to fpeak with you.

*Peach.* Shall we admit her, brother *Lockit?*

*Lock.* By all means——fhe's a good cuftomer, and a fine-fpoken woman —— and a woman who drinks and talks fo freely will enliven the converfation.

*Peach.* Defire her to walk in.                    [*Exit Servant.*

# SCENE VI.

### *PEACHUM, LOCKIT,* Mrs. *TRAPES.*

*Peach.* Dear Mrs. *Dye,* your fervant——one may know by your kifs, that your Ginn is excellent.

*Trapes.* I was always very curious in my liquors.

*Lock.* There is no perfum'd breath like it ——I have been long acquainted with the flavour of thofe lips——han't I, Mrs. *Dye?*

*Trapes.* Fill it up.—— I take as large draughts of liquor, as I did of love.—— I hate a Flincher in either.

AIR

AIR XLVI.    A Shepherd kept sheep, &c.

*In the days of my youth I could bill like a Dove*, fa, la, la, &c.
*Like a Sparrow at all times was ready for love*, fa, la, la, &c.
*The life of all mortals in kissing should pass*,
*Lip to lip while we're young —— then the lip to the glass*, fa, la, &c.

But now, Mr. *Peachum*, to our business. —— If you have blacks of any kind, brought in of late; Mantoes —— Velvet Scarfs — Petticoats — let it be what it will —— I am your chap — for all my ladies are very fond of mourning.

*Peach.* Why, look ye, Mrs. *Dye* —— you deal so hard with us, that we can afford to give the gentlemen, who venture their lives for the goods, little or nothing.

*Trapes.* The hard times oblige me to go very near in my dealing.— To be sure, of late years I have been a great sufferer by the Parliament. —— Three thousand pounds would hardly make me amends.--- The Act for destroying the Mint was a severe cut upon our business ---- 'till then, if a customer stept out of the way —— we knew where to have her —— no doubt you know Mrs. *Coaxer* —— there's a wench now ('till to-day) with a good suit of cloaths of mine upon her back, and I could never set eyes upon her for three months together. —— Since the Act too against imprisonment for small sums, my loss there too hath been very considerable, and it must be so, when a lady can borrow a handsome petticoat, or a clean gown, and I not have the least hank upon her! And, o' my conscience, now-a-days most ladies take a delight in cheating, when they can do it with safety.

*Peach.* Madam, you had a handsome gold watch of us t'other day for seven Guineas. —— Considering we must have our profit —— to a gentleman upon the road, a gold watch will be scarce worth the taking.

*Trap.* Consider, Mr. *Peachum*, that watch was remarkable, and not of very safe sale. —— If you have any black Velvet Scarfs —— they are a handsome winter wear; and take with most gentlemen who deal with my customers. ——'Tis I that put the ladies upon a good foot. 'Tis not youth or beauty that fixes their price. The gentlemen always pay according to their dress, from half a crown to two guineas; and yet those hussies make nothing of bilking of me.— Then too, allowing for accidents. —— I have eleven fine customers

now

now down under the Surgeon's hands, —— what with fees and other expences, there are great goings-out, and no comings-in, and not a farthing to pay for at leaft a month's cloathing. —— We run great rifques ——— great rifques indeed.

*Peach.* As I remember, you faid fomething juft now of Mrs. *Coaxer*.

*Trap.* Yes, Sir. ——To be fure I ftript her of a fuit of my own cloaths about two hours ago; and have left her as fhe fhould be, in her fhift, with a lover of hers at my houfe. She call'd him up ftairs, as he was going to *Marybone* in a hackney-coach. —— And I hope, for her own fake and mine, fhe will perfwade the Captain to redeem her, for the Captain is very generous to the ladies.

*Lock.* What Captain?

*Trap.* He thought I did not know him. —— An intimate acquaintance of yours, Mr. *Peachum* —— only Captain *Macheath* —— as fine as a Lord.

*Peach.* To-morrow, dear Mrs. *Dye*, you fhall fet your own price upon any of the goods you like —— we have at leaft half a dozen Velvet Scarfs, and all at your fervice. Will you give me leave to make you a prefent of this fuit of night-cloaths for your own wearing? ——But are you fure it is Captain *Macheath*?

*Trap.* Though he thinks I have forgot him; no body knows him better. I have taken a great deal of the Captain's money in my time at fecond-hand, for he always lov'd to have his ladies well dreft.

*Peach.* Mr. *Lockit* and I have a little bufinefs with the Captain;—— you underftand me—— and we will fatisfie you for Mrs. *Coaxer*'s debt.

*Lock.* Depend upon it—— we will deal like men of honour.

*Trap.* I don't enquire after your affairs —— fo whatever happens, I wafh my hands on't. —— It hath always been my Maxim, that one friend fhould affift another. —— But if you pleafe —— I'll take one of the Scarfs home with me, 'tis always good to have fomething in hand.

---

# SCENE VII. *Newgate.*

## L U C Y.

Jealoufy, rage, love and fear are at once tearing me to pieces. How I am weather-beaten and fhatter'd with diftreffes!

H                                          A I R

AIR XLVII. One evening having loft my way.

*I'm like a skiff on the Ocean toft,*
*Now high, now low, with each billow born,*
*With her rudder broke, and her anchor loft,*
*Deferted and all forlorn.*
*While thus I lye rolling and toffing all night,*
*That* Polly *lyes fporting on feas of delight!*
*Revenge, revenge, revenge,*
*Shall appeafe my reftlefs fprite.*

I have the Rats-bane ready. —— I run no rifque; for I can lay her death upon the Ginn, and fo many dye of that naturally that I fhall never be call'd in queftion. —— But fay I were to be hang'd —— I never could be hang'd for any thing that would give me greater comfort, than the poyfoning that flut.

*Enter* Filch.
*Filch.* Madam, here's our Mifs *Polly* come to wait upon you.
*Lucy.* Show her in.

## SCENE VIII.

### *L U C Y, P O L L Y.*

*Lucy.* Dear madam, your fervant. —— I hope you will pardon my paffion, when I was fo happy to fee you laft. —— I was fo over-run with the fpleen, that I was perfectly out of my felf. And really when one hath the fpleen, every thing is to be excus'd by a friend.

AIR XLVIII. Now Roger, I'll tell thee, becaufe thou'rt my fon.

*When a wife's in her pout,*
*(As fhe's fometimes, no doubt)*
*The good husband as meek as a lamb,*
*Her vapours to ftill,*
*Firft grants her her will,*
*And the quieting draught is a dram.*
*Poor man! And the quieting draught is a dram.*

—— I

—I wish all our quarrels might have so comfortable a reconciliation.

*Polly.* I have no excuse for my own behaviour, madam, but my misfortunes. — And really, madam, I suffer too upon your account.

*Lucy.* But, Miss *Polly* —— in the way of friendship, will you give me leave to propose a glass of Cordial to you?

*Polly.* Strong-waters are apt to give me the head-ache — I hope, Madam, you will excuse me.

*Lucy.* Not the greatest lady in the land could have better in her closet, for her own private drinking. — You seem mighty low in Spirits, my dear.

*Polly.* I am sorry, madam, my health will not allow me to accept of your offer. —— I should not have left you in the rude manner I did when we met last, madam, had not my Papa haul'd me away so unexpectedly. —— I was indeed somewhat provok'd, and perhaps might use some expressions that were disrespectful. —— But really, madam, the Captain treated me with so much contempt and cruelty, that I deserv'd your pity, rather than your resentment.

*Lucy.* But since his escape, no doubt all matters are made up again. ---- Ah *Polly! Polly!* 'tis I am the unhappy wife; and he loves you as if you were only his mistress.

*Polly.* Sure, madam, you cannot think me so happy as to be the object of your jealousy. ---- A man is always afraid of a woman who loves him too well ---- so that I must expect to be neglected and avoided.

*Lucy.* Then our cases, my dear *Polly*, are exactly alike. Both of us indeed have been too fond.

### AIR XLIX.    O *Bessy Bell*, &c.

| | |
|---|---|
| Polly. | *A curse attends that woman's love* |
| | *Who always would be pleasing.* |
| Lucy. | *The pertness of the billing Dove,* |
| | *Like tickling, is but teazing.* |
| Polly. | *What then in love can woman do?* |
| Lucy. | *If we grow fond they shun us.* |
| Polly. | *And when we fly them, they pursue:* |
| Lucy. | *But leave us when they've won us.* |

*Lucy.* Love is so very whimsical in both sexes, that it is impossible to be lasting. ---- But my heart is particular, and contradicts my own observation.

*Polly.*

*Polly.* But really, miſtreſs *Lucy*, by his laſt behaviour, I think I ought to envy you. —— When I was forc'd from him, he did not ſhew the leaſt tenderneſs. —— But perhaps, he hath a heart not capable of it.

AIR L. Wou'd Fate to me *Belinda* give.

*Among the men, Coquets we find,*
*Who court by turns all woman-kind;*
*And we grant all their hearts deſir'd,*
*When they are flatter'd and admir'd.*

The Coquets of both ſexes are ſelf-lovers, and that is a love no other whatever can diſpoſſeſs. I fear, my dear *Lucy*, our husband is one of thoſe.

*Lucy.* Away with theſe melancholy reflections, —— indeed, my dear *Polly*, we are both of us a cup too low. ---- Let me prevail upon you, to accept of my offer.

AIR LI. Come, ſweet laſs.

*Come, ſweet laſs,*
*Let's baniſh ſorrow*
*'Till to-morrow;*
*Come, ſweet laſs,*
*Let's take a chirping glaſs.*
*Wine can clear*
*The vapours of deſpair;*
*And make us light as air;*
*Then drink, and baniſh care.*

I can't bear, child, to ſee you in ſuch low ſpirits. —— And I muſt perſuade you to what I know will do you good. ---- I ſhall now ſoon be even with the hypocritical Strumpet. [*Aſide.*

---

SCENE IX.

POLLY.

*Polly.* All this wheedling of *Lucy* cannot be for nothing. ---- At this time too! when I know ſhe hates me! ---- The diſſembling of a

woman

woman is always the fore-runner of mischief. — By pouring Strong-waters down my throat, she thinks to pump some secrets out of me — I'll be upon my guard, and won't taste a drop of her liquor, I'm resolv'd.

## SCENE X.

*LUCY, with Strong-waters. POLLY.*

*Lucy.* Come, Miss *Polly.*

*Polly.* Indeed, child, you have given yourself trouble to no purpose. —— You must, my dear, excuse me.

*Lucy.* Really, Miss *Polly*, you are so squeamishly affected about taking a cup of Strong-waters, as a lady before company. I vow, *Polly*, I shall take it monstrously ill if you refuse me. —— Brandy and Men (though women love them never so well) are always taken by us with some reluctance — unless 'tis in private.

*Polly.* I protest, madam, it goes against me. —— What do I see! *Macheath* again in custody! — Now every glimmering of happiness is lost.    [*Drops the glass of liquor on the ground.*

*Lucy.* Since things are thus, I'm glad the wench hath escap'd: for by this event, 'tis plain, she was not happy enough to deserve to be poison'd.

## SCENE XI.

*LOCKIT, MACHEATH, PEACHUM, LUCY, POLLY.*

*Lock.* Set your heart to rest, Captain. —— You have neither the chance of Love or Money for another escape —— for you are order'd to be call'd down upon your Tryal immediately.

*Peach.* Away, hussies! —— This is not a time for a man to be hamper'd with his wives. —— You see, the gentleman is in chains already.

*Lucy.* O husband, husband, my heart long'd to see thee; but to see thee thus distracts me!

*Polly.* Will not my dear husband look upon his *Polly?* Why hadst thou not flown to me for protection? with me thou hadst been safe.

AIR

### AIR LII.   The laſt time I went o'er the Moor.

| | |
|---|---|
| Polly. | *Hither, dear husband, turn your eyes.* |
| Lucy. | *Beſtow one glance to cheer me.* |
| Polly. | *Think with that look, thy* Polly *dyes.* |
| Lucy. | *O ſhun me not, — but hear me.* |
| Polly. | *'Tis* Polly *ſues.* |
| Lucy. | —————— *'Tis* Lucy *ſpeaks.* |
| Polly. | *Is thus true love requited?* |
| Lucy. | *My heart is burſting.* |
| Polly. | ——— ——— *Mine too breaks.* |
| Lucy. | *Muſt I,* |
| Polly. | ——————— *Muſt I be ſlighted?* |

*Mach.* What would you have me ſay, ladies? ——— You ſee, this affair will ſoon be at an end, without my diſobliging either of you.

*Peach.* But the ſettling this point, Captain, might prevent a Lawſuit between your two widows.

### AIR LIII.   *Tom Tinker's my true love, &c.*

*Mach.* *Which way ſhall I turn me —— how can I decide?*
*Wives, the day of our death, are as fond as a bride.*
*One wife is too much for moſt husbands to hear,*
*But two at a time there's no mortal can bear.*
*This way, and that way, and which way I will,*
*What would comfort the one, t'other wife would take ill.*

*Polly.* But if his own misfortunes have made him inſenſible to mine —— a Father ſure will be more compaſſionate. ——— Dear, dear Sir, ſink the material evidence, and bring him off at his Tryal— *Polly* upon her knees begs it of you.

### AIR LIV.   I am a poor Shepherd undone.

*When my Hero in court appears,*
*    And ſtands arraign'd for his life,*
*Then think of poor* Polly's *tears;*
*    For ah! poor* Polly's *his wife.*

*Like*

*Like the Sailor he holds up his hand,*
   *Diſtreſt on the daſhing wave.*
*To die a dry death at land,*
   *Is as bad as a watry grave.*
*And alas, poor* Polly *!*
*Alack, and well-a-day !*
*Before I was in love,*
   *Oh ! every month was* May.

*Lucy.* If *Peachum*'s heart is harden'd ; ſure you, Sir, will have more compaſſion on a daughter. —— I know the evidence is in your power. —— How then can you be a tyrant to me?   [*Kneeling.*

### AIR LV.   *Ianthe the lovely, &c.*

*When he holds up his hand arraign'd for his life,*
*O think of your daughter, and think I'm his wife !*
*What are cannons, or bombs, or claſhing of ſwords ?*
*For death is more certain by witneſſes words.*
*Then nail up their lips ; that dread thunder allay ;*
*And each month of my life will hereafter be* May.

*Lock. Macheath*'s time is come, *Lucy.* —— We know our own affairs, therefore let us have no more whimpering or whining.

### AIR LVI.   *A Cobler there was, &c.*

*Our ſelves, like the Great, to ſecure a retreat,*
*When matters require it, muſt give up our gang :*
   *And good reaſon why,*
   *Or, inſtead of the fry,*
   *Ev'n* Peachum *and I,*
*Like poor petty raſcals, might hang, hang ;*
*Like poor petty raſcals, might hang.*

*Peach.* Set your heart at reſt, *Polly.* —— Your husband is to dye to-day. —— Therefore, if you are not already provided, 'tis high time to look about for another. There's comfort for you, you ſlut.

*Lock.* We are ready, Sir, to conduct you to the *Old Baily.*

AIR

AIR LVII. Bonny *Dundee*.

*Mach.* *The charge is prepar'd ; the Lawyers are met ;*
*The Judges all rang'd (a terrible show !)*
*I go, undismay'd. ——— For death is a debt,*
*A debt on demand. ——— So, take what I owe.*
*Then farewell, my love —— dear charmers, adieu.*
*Contented I die ———'tis the better for you.*
*Here ends all dispute the rest of our lives,*
*For this way at once I please all my wives.*

Now, Gentlemen, I am ready to attend you.

## SCENE XII.

*LUCY, POLLY, FILCH.*

*Polly.* Follow them, *Filch*, to the Court.   And when the Tryal is over, bring me a particular account of his behaviour, and of every thing that happen'd. ——— You'll find me here with Miss *Lucy*. [*Ex.* Filch.] But why is all this Musick?

*Lucy.* The Prisoners, whose tryals are put off till next Session, are diverting themselves.

*Polly.* Sure there is nothing so charming as Musick! I'm fond of it to distraction ——— But alas! —— now, all mirth seems an insult upon my affliction. ——— Let us retire, my dear *Lucy*, and indulge our sorrows. —— The noisy crew, you see, are coming upon us. [*Exeunt.*
*A Dance of Prisoners in chains,* &c.

## SCENE XIII.    *The Condemn'd Hold.*

*MACHEATH, in a melancholy posture.*

### AIR LVIII. Happy Groves.

*O cruel, cruel, cruel case!*
*Must I suffer this disgrace?*

### AIR LIX.   Of all the girls that are so smart.

*Of all the friends in time of grief,*
*When threatning Death looks grimmer,*
*Not one so sure can bring relief,*
*As this best friend a brimmer.*

[Drinks.
AIR

### AIR LX.    *Britons* strike home.

*Since I must swing, ---- I scorn, I scorn to wince or whine.*    [Rises.

### AIR LXI.    Chevy Chase.

*But now again my spirits sink;*
*I'll raise them high with wine.*        [Drinks a glass of wine.

### AIR LXII.    To old Sir *Simon* the King.

*But valour the stronger grows,*
*    The stronger liquor we're drinking.*
*And how can we feel our woes,*
*    When we've lost the trouble of thinking?*        [Drinks.

### AIR LXIII.    Joy to great *Cæsar*.

*If thus ---- A man can die*
*Much bolder with brandy.*    [Pours out a bumper of brandy.

### AIR LXIV.    There was an old woman, *&c.*

*So I drink off this bumper ---- And now I can stand the test,*
*And my Comrades shall see, that I die as brave as the best.* [Drinks.

### AIR LXV.    Did you ever hear of a gallant sailor.

*    But can I leave my pretty hussies,*
*    Without one tear, or tender sigh?*

### AIR LXVI.    Why are mine eyes still flowing.

*    Their eyes, their lips, their busses*
*    Recall my love ---- Ah must I die!*

### AIR LXVII.    Green sleeves.

*Since laws were made for ev'ry degree,*
*To curb vice in others, as well as me,*
*I wonder we han't better company*
*    Upon* Tyburn *tree!*

I

*But*

*But gold from law can take out the sting;*
*And if rich men like us were to swing,*
*'Twou'd thin the land, such numbers to string*
*Upon* Tyburn *tree!*

*Jailor.* Some friends of yours, Captain, desire to be admitted—— I leave you together.

---

## SCENE XIV.

### *MACHEATH, BEN BUDGE, MAT of the Mint.*

*Mach.* For my having broke Prison, you see, gentlemen, I am order'd immediate execution.—— The Sheriffs officers, I believe, are now at the door.—— That *Jemmy Twitcher* should peach me, I own surpriz'd me!—'Tis a plain proof that the world is all alike, and that even our Gang can no more trust one another than other people. Therefore, I beg you, gentlemen, look well to your selves, for in all probability you may live some months longer.

*Mat.* We are heartily sorry, Captain, for your misfortune.—But 'tis what we must all come to.

*Mach. Peachum* and *Lockit,* you know, are infamous Scoundrels. Their lives are as much in your power, as yours are in theirs—— Remember your dying friend!—— 'Tis my last request.—— Bring those villains to the Gallows before you, and I am satisfied.

*Mat.* We'll do't.

*Jailor.* Miss *Polly* and Miss *Lucy* intreat a word with you.

*Mach.* Gentlemen, adieu.

---

## SCENE XV.

### *LUCY, MACHEATH, POLLY.*

*Mach.* My dear *Lucy* ----- my dear *Polly* ----- Whatsoever hath past between us is now at an end. ---- If you are fond of marrying again, the best advice I can give you, is to ship yourselves off for the *West-Indies,* where you'll have a fair chance of getting a husband a-piece; or by good luck, two or three, as you like best.

*Polly.* How can I support this sight!

*Lucy.* There is nothing moves one so much as a great man in distress.

AIR

### AIR LXVIII.    All you that muſt take a leap, &c.

Lucy.    *Would I might be hang'd!*
Polly.    - - - - - - - - - - - - *And I would ſo too!*
Lucy.    *To be hang'd with you,*
Polly.    - - - - - - - - - - *My dear, with you.*
Mach.    *O leave me to thought! I fear! I doubt!*
*I tremble! I droop!* - - - - *See, my courage is out.*
        [Turns up the empty bottle.
Polly.    *No token of love?*
Mach.    - - - - - - - - *See, my courage is cut.*
        [Turns up the empty pot.
Lucy.    *No token of love?*
Polly.    - - - - - - - - *Adieu.*
Lucy.    - - - - - - - - - - - *Farewell.*
Mach.    *But hark! I hear the toll of the bell.*
Chorus.        *Tol de rol lol,* &c.

*Jailor.* Four women more, Captain, with a child a-peice! See, here they come.        [*Enter women and children.*

*Mach.* What - - - - four wives more! - - - - This is too much. - - - - Here — tell the Sheriffs officers I am ready.    [*Exit* Macheath *guarded.*

---

## SCENE XVI.

*To them, Enter* PLAYER *and* BEGGAR.

*Play.* But, honeſt friend, I hope you don't intend that *Macheath* ſhall be really executed.

*Beg.* Moſt certainly, Sir. - - - - To make the piece perfect, I was for doing ſtrict poetical Juſtice. - - - - *Macheath* is to be hang'd; and for the other perſonages of the Drama, the Audience muſt have ſuppos'd they were all either hang'd or tranſported.

*Play.* Why then, friend, this is a down-right deep Tragedy. The cataſtrophe is manifeſtly wrong, for an Opera muſt end happily.

*Beg.* Your objection, Sir, is very juſt; and is eaſily remov'd. For you muſt allow, that in this kind of Drama, 'tis no matter how abſurdly things are brought about - - - - So - - - you rabble there - - - - run and cry a Reprieve - - - - let the priſoner be brought back to his wives in triumph.
                                    *Play.*

*Play.* All this we muſt do, to comply with the taſte of the town.

*Beg.* Through the whole piece you may obſerve ſuch a ſimilitude of manners in high and low life, that it is difficult to determine whe- ther (in the faſhionable vices) the fine gentlemen imitate the gentle- men of the road, or the gentlemen of the road the fine gentlemen.---- Had the Play remain'd, as I at firſt intended, it would have carried a moſt excellent moral. 'Twould have ſhown that the lower ſort of people have their vices in a degree as well as the rich : And that they are puniſh'd for them.

## SCENE XVII.

*To them MACHEATH with Rabble, &c.*

*Mach.* So, it ſeems, I am not left to my choice, but muſt have a wife at laſt. ——Look ye, my dears, we will have no controverſie now. Let us give this day to mirth, and I am ſure ſhe who thinks her ſelf my wife will teſtifie her joy by a dance.

*All.* Come, a Dance——a Dance.

*Mach.* Ladies, I hope you will give me leave to preſent a Partner to each of you. And (if I may without offence) for this time, I take *Polly* for mine. --- And for life, you ſlut, --- for we were really marry'd. ---- As for the reſt. ---- But at preſent keep your own ſecret.

[*To Polly.*

### A DANCE.

**AIR LXIX.** Lumps of Pudding, *&c.*

*Thus I ſtand like the* Turk, *with his doxies around ;*
*From all ſides their glances his paſſion confound ;*
*For black, brown, and fair, his inconſtancy burns,*
*And the different beauties ſubdue him by turns :*
*Each calls forth her charms, to provoke his deſires :*
*Though willing to all; with but one he retires.*
*But think of this maxim, and put off your ſorrow,*
*The wretch of to-day, may be happy to-morrow.*

Chorus. *But think of this maxim, &c.*

# FINIS.

# OUVERTURE in SCORE

## Compos'd by Dr. *PEPUSCH*.

A

# The OUVERTURE.

*the Repeat pia:*

# The OUVERTURE.

# The OUVERTURE

# The OUVERTURE

# SONGS in the BEGGAR's OPERA.

## A C T I.

### AIR I. An old woman cloathed in gray.

Thro' all the employments of life. Each neighbour a-bu-ses his

brother; Whore and Rogue they call Husband and Wife: All professions be=

=rogue one a=nother.The Priest calls the Lawyer a cheat,The Lawyer beknaves the Di=

=vine; And the Statesman, because he's so great, Thinks his trade as honest as mine.

### AIR II. The bonny gray-ey'd morn. &c.

'Tis Woman that se=duces all mankind,By her we first were taught the

B

wheedling Arts: Her very eyes can cheat; when most she's kind, She tricks us

of our money with our hearts. For her like Wolves by night we roam for prey, And

practise ev'ry fraud to bribe her charms; For suits of Love, like Law, are

won by pay, And beauty must be fee'd into our arms.

## AIR III. Cold and raw, &c.

If any wench Venus's girdle near, Though she be never so ugly;

Lillies and roses will quickly appear; And her face look wondrous smuggly. Be=

=neath the left ear so fit but a cord, (A rope so charming a Zone is!) The

Youth in his cart hath the air of a Lord, And we cry, There dies an Adonis!

## AIR IV. Why is your faithful slave disdain'd?

If Love the Virgin's heart in = vade, How, like a Moth, the simple Maid

Still plays a--bout the flame! If soon ---she be not made a Wife, Her

Honour's sing'd, and then for life, she's what I dare not name.

## AIR V. Of all the simple things we do.

A Maid is like the golden oar, Which hath guineas intrinsical in't, Whose

worth is never known, before It is try'd and imprest in the Mint. A

Wife's like a guinea in gold, Stampt with the name of her Spouse; Now

here, now there; is bought, or is sold; And is current in every house.

AIR VI. What shall I do to shew how much I love her.

Virgins are like the fair flow'r in its lustre, Which in the garden e=

=namels the ground; Near it the Bees in play flutter & cluster, & gaudy Butterflies

frolick around. But, when once pluckt, 'tis no longer al=luring, to Covent=

=Garden 'tis sent, (as yet sweet,) There fades, and shrinks, and grows

past all en=during, Rots, stinks, & dies, & is trod under feet.

AIR VII. Oh London is a fine town.

Our Polly is a sad slut.' nor heeds what we have taught her. I wonder any

man alive will ever rear a Daughter! For she must have both hoods and gowns, and

hoops to swell her pride, With scarfs and stays, and gloves and lace; and she will have men be=

=side; And when she's drest with care and cost, all-tempting, fine and gay, As

men should serve a Cowcumber, she flings her self away.

AIR VIII. Grim King of the ghosts, &c.

Can Love be controul'd by advice? Will Cupid our Mothers o=

=bey? Though my heart were as frozen as Ice, At his flame 'twould have melted a=

=way. When he kist me so closely he prest, 'Twas so sweet that I must have comply'd: So I thought it both safest and best To marry, for fear you should chide.

AIR IX. O Jenny, O Jenny, where hast thou been?

O Polly, you might have toy'd and kist. By keeping men off, you keep them on.

But he so teaz'd me, And he so pleas'd me, What I did, you must have done.

AIR X. Thomas, I cannot, &c.

I, like a Ship in storms, was tost; Yet afraid to put in to land; For

seiz'd in the port the vessel's lost, Whose treasure is contreband. The

waves are laid, My du-ty's paid. O Joy beyond Expres-sion! Thus safe ashore, I

ask no more, My all is in my possession, possession, My all is in my possession.

AIR XI. A soldier and a sailor

A fox may steal your hens, Sir, A whore your health and pence, Sir, Your

daughter rob your chest, Sir, Your wife may steal your rest, Sir, A thief your goods and

Plate. A Thief your Goods & Plate. But this is

all but Picking, With rest, pence, chest & chicken; It e = ver

was decreed, Sir, If Law = yer's hand is feed Sir, he Steals your whole Es=

:tate. he Steals your whole Estate

AIR XII. Now ponder well, ye parents dear.

Oh, ponder well! be not severe; So save a wretched

wife! For on the rope that hangs my Dear, depends poor Polly's life.

**AIR XIII.   Le printemps rappelle aux armes.**

The Turtle thus with Plaintive crying, her lover = dying,

The Turtle thus with Plaintive crying, La = ments her Dove. Down she

drops quite Spent with Sighing, Paird in death, as = paird in Love.

**AIR XIV.   Pretty Parrot, say.**

Pretty Polly, say, When I was away, Did your fancy never

Stray to some newer Lo = ver? Without Disguise, = Heaving

Sighs, = Doating Eyes, My constant heart discover. Fond =

= ly let me loll! Fond = ly let me loll! O Pretty, Pretty Poll.

### AIR XV. Pray fair one be kind, &c.

My heart was so free, It rov'd like the Bee, 'Till Polly my passion requited:

I sipt each Flow'r, I chang'd ev'ry hour; I sipt each flow'r, I

chang'd ev'ry hour    But here ev'ry    Flower's u = nited.

### AIR XVI. Over the hills and far away.

Were I laid on Greenland's coast, And in my arms embrac'd my lass: Warm a=

= midst eternal frost, Too soon the half year's night would pass. Were I sold on

Indian soil, Soon as the burning day was clos'd, I could mock the Sultry toil, When

C

on my charmer's breast repos'd. And I would love you all the day, Every night would

kiss and play. If with me you'd fondly stray O ver the hills and far away.

AIR XVII. Gin thou wert mine awn thing:

O what pain it is to part! Can I leave thee, can I leave thee?

O what pain it is to part! Can thy Polly ever leave thee?

But lest death my love shoud thwart, & bring thee to the fa = tal Cart, Thus I

tear thee from my bleeding heart! Fly hence, & let me leave thee

AIR XVIII. O the broom, &c.

The Miser thus a shilling sees, Which he's oblig'd to pay, With sighs resigns it by degrees, And fears 'tis gone for aye. The Boy, tho'when his

Sparrow's flown, The bird in silence eyes; But soon as out of

sight 'tis gone, Whines, whimpers, sobs and cries.

*End of the First Act.*

C 2

## ACT II.

### AIR XIX. Fill ev'ry glass &c

Fill e'ry glass, for Wine inspires us, And fires us, With courage, love &

joy. Women and wine should life employ, Is there ought elsc on earth de-si-rous

Da Cap.

### AIR XX March in Rinaldo, with drums and trumpets

Let us take the road, Hark! I hear the sound of coaches! The

hour of attack approaches, To your arms brave boys and load. See the Ball I

hold! Let the Chymists toil like asses Our fire their fire sur-

=passes, And turns all our lead to gold.

## AIR XXI. Wou'd you have a young Virgin, &c.

If the heart of a man is deprest with cares, The mist is dispell'd when a

woman appears; Like the notes of a fiddle, she sweetly, sweetly Raises the

spirits and charms our ears. Roses and lillies her cheeks disclose But her ripe

lips are more sweet than those. Press her, Caress her With blisses her kisses dis=

=solve us in pleasure, and soft repose

## AIR XXII. Cotillon

Youth's the season made for joys, Love is then our Duty; She alone who

that employs, Well deserves her beauty, Let's be gay, While we may, Beauty's a flower despis'd in decay. Youth's the Season made for Joys, Love is then our

duty. Let us drink and sport to-day, Ours is not to-morrow. Love with Youth flies

Swift away, Age is nought but Sorrow. Dance and sing, Time's on the wing, Life never

knows the return of Spring. Let us drink and sport to day, Ours is not to-morrow.

### AIR XXIII. All in a misty morning, &c.

Before the barn-door crowing, the Cock by Hens attended, His eyes around him

throwing, Stands for a while suspended. Then one he singles from the crew, and

cheers the happy Hen; With how d'you do, and how d'you do, And how d'you do again.

AIR XXIV. When once I lay with another man's wife.

The Gamesters and Lawyers are jugglers alike, If they meddle your all is in

danger. Like Gypsies, if once they can finger a souse, Your pockets they pick, and they

pilfer your house. And give your estate to a stranger.

AIR XXV. When first I laid siege to my Chloris.

At the Tree I shall suffer with pleasure: Let me go where I will. In

all kinds of ill, I shall find no such Furies as these are.

AIR XXVI. Courtiers, Courtiers, think it no harm.

Man may escape from rope and gun; Nay, some have out-liv'd the

Doctor's pill: Who takes a woman must be undone, that Basi= lisk is

sure to kill. The Fly that sips Treacle is lost in the sweets, so

he that tastes Woman, Woman, Woman, he that tastes Woman, ruin meets.

AIR XXVII. A lovely lass to a Friar came.

Thus when a good huswife sees a Rat in her trap in the morning taken,

With pleasure her heart goes pit a pat, In revenge for her loss of bacon. Then she

throws him To the Dog or Cat, To be worried, crush'd and shaken.

AIR XXVIII. 'Twas when the Sea was roaring.

How cruel are the traytors, Who lye and swear in jest, To cheat un=

=guarded creatures Of virtue, fame, and rest! Whoever steals a shilling, Thro'

shame the guilt conceals: In love the perjur'd villain With boasts the theft reveals.

AIR XXIX. The Sun had loos'd his weary teams.

The first time at the looking-glass The mother sets her daughter; The

Image strikes the smiling lass With self-love ever after. Each

time she looks, she, fonder grown, Thinks ev'ry charm grows stronger: But a-

las, vain maid, all eyes but your own Can see you are not younger.

AIR XXX. How happy are we, &c.

When you censure the age, Be cautious and sage, Lest the Courtiers of-

= fended shou'd be: If you mention Vice or bribe, 'Tis so

D

pat to all the Tribe each crys that was levell'd at me.

### AIR XXXI. Of a noble race was *Shenkin*.

*Vio:*

Is then his fate decreed Sir? - - - -

*Vio:*

Such a Man can I think of quitting? When

first we met so moves me yet, O see how my heart is splitting!

### AIR XXXII.

You'll think, e'er many days ensue, This sentence not severe; I hang your

husband, child, 'tis true, But with him hang your care. Twang dang dillo dee.

### AIR XXXIII. *London* Ladies.

If you at an Office solicit your due, And would not have matters neg=

AIR XXXIV. All in the Downs, &c.

AIR XXXV.   Have you heard of a frolicksome ditty.

*How happy could I be with either, Were t'other dear charmer away! But*

*while you thus teaze me together, To neither a word will I say; But tol de rol, &c.*

AIR XXXVI.   Irish Trot.

*I'm bubbled. I'm bubbled. Oh how I am troubled! Bambouzled, and*

*bit! My distresses are doubled. When you come to the Tree, should the Hangman re-*

*=fuse These fingers, with pleasure, could fasten the noose. I'm bubbled, &c.*

AIR XXXVII.

*Cease your funning; Force or cunning, Never shall my heart trapan.*

*All these sallies Are but malice To seduce my constant man.'Tis most certain,*

By their flirting Women oft have envy shonn: Pleas'd, to ruin Others wooing;

Never happy in their onn.

**AIR XXXVIII.** Good morow, Goſſip *Joan.*

Why how non; Madam Flirt, If ---- you this must chatter;

And are for flinging Dir - - - - - - - - - - - t, Let's

try who best can ſpat = = ter; Madam Flirt. Why how non; Saucy

Jade! Sure the Wench is Tipsey. How can you see me made =

- - - - - - - The ſcoff of ſuch a Gip = ſey? Saucy Jade!

# SONGS in the BEGGAR's OPERA.

## AIR XXX. How happy are, &c..

No pow'r on earth can e'er divide, The knot that sacred Love hath ty'd.

When parents draw against our mind, The true-love's knot they faster bind, Ho ho ra in

ambo = ra = ho an ho derry hi an hi derry

hoo hoo derry derry derry Derry ambo = ra — — — —

## AIR XL. The Lass of Patie's Mill, &c.

I like the Fox shall grieve, Whose mate hath left her side, Whom

Hounds, from morn to eve, Chase o'er the country wide. Where can my lover

hide? Where cheat the wary pack? If Love be not his guide, He never will come back!

*End of the Second Act.*

## A C T   III.
### AIR XLI. If Love's a sweet passion &c.

When young at the bar you first taught me to score, And bid me be free of my

lips, and no more; I was kiss'd by the Parson, the Squire, and the Sot: When the

guest was departed, the kiss was forgot. But his kiss was so sweet, and so

closely he prest. That I languish'd and pin'd 'till I granted the rest.

### AIR XLII. South Sea Ballad.

My love is all madness and folly, alone I lye, toss, tumble and

cry, What a happy creature is Polly! = Was e'er such a wretch as

I - - - With rage I redsen like scarlet, - That my dear in =

= con = stant Varlet— Stark blind to my charms, is lost in the

arms Of that Jilt, that inveigling) Harlot! Stark blind to my charms, is

lost in the arms Of that Jilt, that inveigling) Harlot! This, this my re =

= Sentiment alarms.

AIR XLIII. Packington's Pound.

Thus Gamesters united in friendship are found, Though they know that their

industry all is a cheat; They flock to their prey at the Dice box's sound, And

join to promote one another's deceit. But if by mishap They fail of a chap; To

keep in their hands, they each other entrap. Like Pikes, lank with hunger, who

miss of their ends, They bite their companions, and prey on their friends.

## AIR XLIV. Lillibulero.

The modes of the Court so common are grown, That a true friend can

hardly be met; Friendship for interest is but a loan, Which they let out for

what they can get: 'Tis true, you find Some friends so kind, Who'll give you good

counsel themselves to defend. In sorrowful ditty, They promise, they

E

pity, But shift you for money from friend to friend.

**AIR XLV. Down in the North Country.**

What Gudgeons are we Men Ev'ry Woman's easy Prey. Tho' we have felt the

Hook, agen = = We bite and they betray. The Bird that has been

trapt, when he hears his calling Mate: To her he flies, a = gain he's

clapt = = within the Wiry Grate:

**AIR XLVI. A Shepherd kept sheep, &c.**

In the Days of my youth I could bill like a Dove fa la la

fa &c.     In the days of my youth I cou'd bill like a Dove, Like a

lorn, While thus I lye rolling and tossing all Night, That Polly lyes

Sporting on Seas of Delight; Revenge, revenge, revenge, shall ap........

peace my restless Sprite.

**AIR XLVIII.** Now *Roger*, I'll tell thee, because thou'rt my Son.

When a wife's in her pout, as she's sometimes no doubt; The good

husband as meek as a lamb, Her vapours to still, first grants her her will, & the

quieting draught is a dram, Poor man! and the quieting draught is a dram.

**AIR XLIX.** O *Bessy Bell* &c.

A curse attends that woman's love, Who always would be pleasing. The

pertness of the billing Dove, Like tickling is but teazing. What then in love can

woman do? If we grow fond they shun us, And when we fly them,

they pursue; But leave us when they've won us.

**AIR L. Wou'd Fate to me *Belinda* give.**

Among the men, Coquets we find, Who court by turns all Wo==man=

=kind; And we grant all their hearts desir'd, When they are flatter'd,

when they are flatter'd, when they are flatter'd, and admir'd.

**AIR LI. Come, sweet lass**

Come sweet lass, Let's banish sorrow, Till to-morrow: Come, sweet lass, Lets

take a chirping Glass, Wine can clear the vapours of despair; And make us light as

air; then drink and ba-nish care.

AIR LII. The last time I went o'er the Moor.

Hither dear husband, turn your eyes Bestow one glance to cheer me, Think

with that look thy Polly dyes, O shun me not but hear me. 'Tis Polly sues, 'Tis

Lucy speaks. Is thus true love requited? My heart is bursting. Mine too

breaks, Must I, must I be Slight = = ed.

AIR LIII. Tom Tinker's my true love &c.

Which way shall I turn me, how can I decide? Wives the day of our

Death are as fond as a Bride: One Wife is too much for most husbands to

hear; but two at a time there's no Mortal can bear. This way, and

that way, and which way I will, What woud comfort the one t'other wife woud take ill.

### AIR LIV. I am a poor Shepherd undone.

When my hero in court appears, And stands arraign'd for his life; Then

think of poor Polly's tears; For ah! Poor Polly's his wife. Like the Sailor he

holds up his hand, Distrest on the dashing wave. To die a dry death at land, Is as

bad as a watry grave. And alas, poor Polly! Alack, and well-a-day! Before I

'was in love, Oh! every month was May.

**AIR LV.** *Ianthe the lovely, &c.*

When he holds up his hand arraign'd for his life, O think of your

daughter, and think I'm his wife! What are cannons, or bombs, or clashing of

swords? For death is more certain by witnesses words. Then nail up their lips; that dread

thunder allay; And each month of my life, And each month of my Life will here=

=after be May.

**AIR LVI.** A Cobler there was, &c.

ourselves, like the great, to secure a retreat; When matters re=

=quire it, muſt give up our gang : And good reaſon why, Or, inſtead of the fry, Ev'n

Peachum and I, Like poor petty raſcals, might hang, hang ; Like

poor petty raſcals, might hang.

AIR LVII. Bonny Dundee.

The charge is prepar'd ; the Lawyers are met ; The Judges all rang'd (a

terrible ſhow !) ſ go, undiſmay'd. For death is a debt, A debt on demand. So,

take what I owe. Then farewell, my love ; dear charmers, adieu. Contented I die; 'tis the

better for you. Here ends all diſpute the reſt of our lives. For this way at

F

once I please all my wives.

AIR LVIII. Happy Groves.

O cruel, cruel, cruel case! Must I suffer this disgrace?

AIR LIX. Of all the girls that are so smart.

Of all the friends in time of grief, When threatning death looks grimmer,=

Not one so sure can bring relief, As this best friend a brimmer.

AIR LX. Britons strike Home.

Since I must swing,--I scorn, I scorn to wince or whine.

AIR LXI. Chevy Chase.

But now again my spirits sink, I'll raise them high with wine.

AIR LXII. To old Sir Simon the King.

But valour the stronger grows, The stronger liquor we're drinking. And how can we feel our woes, When we've lost the trouble of thinking?

**AIR LXIII.** Joy to great Cæsar.

If thus A man can die Much bolder with brandy.

**AIR LXIV.** There was an old woman, &c.

So I drink off this bumper And now I can stand the test: And my

Comrades shall see, that I die as brave as the best.

**AIR LXV.** Did you ever hear of a gallant sailor.

But can I leave my pretty hussies, without one tear, or tender Sigh?

**AIR LXVI.** Why are mine eyes still flowing.

Their eyes, their lips, their Bus = = =ses recall my love. Ah

must I die!

AIR LXVII. Green sleeves.

*Since laws were made for ev'ry degree, To curb vice in others, as*

*well as me, I wonder we han't better company, Upon Ty — — burn Tree!*

*But Gold from law can take out the Sting; And if rich men like us were to*

*swing, 'Twou'd thin the Land, such Numbers to string upon Ty — — burn Tree!*

AIR LXVIII.   All you that must take a leap, &c.

*Would I might be hang'd! And I would so too! To be hang'd with*

*you, My dear, with you, O leave me to thought! I fear! I doubt! I tremble! I*

*droop! See, my. courage is out. No token of love? See my courage is out. No token of*

love? A-dieu. Farewell. No token of love? Adieu: Farewell, But hark! I

hear - - the Toll of the Bell.

**AIR LXIX.** Lumps of Pudding, &c.

Thus I stand like the Turk, with his Doxies around; From all sides their

Glances his Passion confound; For black, brown, and fair, his Inconstancy

burns: And the different Beauties subdue him by turns.

Violins

Each calls forth her charms, to provoke his desires; Tho'

G

willing to all; with but one he retires. But think of this Maxim, and

put off all Sorrow, The Wretch of to day, may be happy to morrow.

Each calls forth her charms, to pro=

=voke his desires. Tho' willing to all, with but one he retires. - But

think of this Maxim, and put off all Sorrow, The wretch of to day, may be

happy to Morrow.

*FINIS.*

# THE SOURCES OF THE SONGS IN

## *THE BEGGAR'S OPERA*

## BY MAX GOBERMAN

All of the songs in *The Beggar's Opera* were adapted by John Gay from popular songs and ballads of his time. On the following pages may be seen side by side Gay's verses and equivalent portions of the original songs he adapted. Gay's verses are printed on the left exactly as they appear in the text of *The Beggar's Opera*, except that where lines or phrases are repeated for musical purposes in the score, they are given here within brackets. The original words are printed on the right exactly as they are found in the contemporary or later song collections named.

It was the fashion of the day to take existing songs and decorate them musically in various ways. In some cases, therefore, the reader may have difficulty matching the original words with the tunes as Gay used them. However, most of these songs reveal quite clearly the connotations Gay's versions had for the audience of 1728.

The sources referred to are the following:

D'URFEY, THOMAS. *Wit and Mirth: or Pills to Purge Melancholy; being a collection of the best merry Ballads and Songs, old and new. Fitted to all Humours, having each their proper tune for either voice, or Instrument: Most of the songs being new set.* 6 volumes. London: 1719-20.

THOMSON, WILLIAM. *Orpheus Caledonius: or, a Collection of Scots Songs. Set to Musick by W. Thomson.* London: 1725-26.

WATTS, JOHN. *The Musical Miscellany; being a collection of choice songs, and Lyrick Poems: By the most Eminent Masters.* 6 volumes. Printed by and for John Watts. London: 1729-31.

CHAPPELL, WILLIAM. *The Ballad Literature and Popular Music of the Olden Time: A history of the ancient songs, ballads, and of the dance tunes of England, with numerous anecdotes and entire ballads. Also a short account of the minstrels.* London: Chappell & Co. (1855-59)

PLAYFORD, HENRY. *The Banquet of Musick.* London: 1688.

PLAYFORD, JOHN. *The Dancing Master.* This work appeared in so many editions over a long period of time, that it is futile to allocate the songs to particular dates, and impossible to give bibliographical data here.

──────── AIR I.   An old woman cloathed in gray. ────────

Through all the employments of life
Each neighbour abuses his brother;
Whore and Rogue they call Husband
      and Wife:
All professions be-rogue one another.
The Priest calls the Lawyer a cheat,
The Lawyer be-knaves the Divine;
And the Statesman, because he's so great,
Thinks his trade as honest as mine.

An old woman cloathed in grey
Whose daughter was charming and young
But chanc'd to be once led
      astray,
By Rogers false flattering Tongue
With whom she too often had been,
Abroad in the meadows and Fields.

*The Dancing Master*

──────── AIR II.   The bonny gray-ey'd morn, &c. ────────

'Tis woman that seduces all mankind,
By her we first were taught the wheedling arts:
Her very eyes can cheat; when most she's kind,
She tricks us of our money with our hearts.
For her, like Wolves by night we roam for prey,
And practise ev'ry fraud to bribe her charms;
For suits of love, like law, are won by pay,
And Beauty must be fee'd into our arms.

(2nd stanza)

Upon my bosom Jockey laid his head,
And sighing told me pretty Tales of Love;
My yielding heart at ev'ry word he said,
Did flutter up and down and strangely move:
He sigh'd, he Kissed my Hand, he vow'd and swore,
That I had o'er his Heart a Conquest gain'd;
Then Blushing begg'd that I would grant him more,
Which he, alass! too soon, too soon obtain'd.

*Pills to Purge Melancholy* – Vol. III

──────── AIR III.   Cold and raw, &c. ────────

If any wench Venus's girdle wear,
Though she be never so ugly,
Lillies and roses will quickly appear,
And her face look wond'rous smuggly.
Beneath the left ear so fit* but a cord,
(A rope so charming a Zone is!)
The youth in his cart hath the air of a lord,
And we cry, There dies an Adonis!

Cold and Raw the North did Blow,
Bleak in the Morning early;
All the Trees were hid in Snow,
Dagl'd by Winter yearly:
When come Riding over a Knough,
I met with a Farmer's Daughter;
Rosie Cheeks and bonny Brow,
Good faith made my Mouth to Water.

*The word "sit" in the score is evidently a typographical error.        *Pills to Purge Melancholy* – Vol. II

The words of the original are by D'Urfey. It has also been called "The Farmer's Daughter", "The Scotchman outwitted by the Farmer's Daughter", and "A Little of one with t'other". An anecdote connected with this song tells of a Mrs. Arabella Hunt who was singing for Queen Mary. Her accompanist at the harpsichord was Henry Purcell. When the Queen asked Mrs. Hunt if she could sing "Cold and Raw", Purcell was somewhat nettled to have to sit idle at the harpsichord while the song was being sung because he did not know it. He later (1892) used the tune as the bass for "May her bright example chace vice in troops out of the land" in a birthday ode he wrote for Queen Mary.

——————— AIR IV. Why is your faithful slave disdain'd? ———————

If love the virgin's heart invade,
How, like a Moth, the simple maid
Still plays about the flame!
If soon she be not made a wife,
Her honour's sing'd, and then for life,
She's—what I dare not name.

Why is your faithful Slave disdain'd
By gentle Arts my Heart you gain'd!
Oh! keep it by the same!
For ever shall my Passion last,
If you will make me once possest,
Of what I dare not name.

*The Banquet of Musick*

The similarity of last lines in Gay's song and the original was probably not lost on the listeners. The air was by Bononcini, composer of many Italian operas.

——————— AIR V. Of all the simple things we do, &c. ———————

A Maid is like the golden oar,
Which hath guineas intrinsical in't,
Whose worth is never known, before
It is try'd and imprest in the mint.
A Wife's like a guinea in gold,
Stampt with the name of her spouse;
Now here, now there; is bought, or is sold;
And is current in every house.

Of all the simple things we do,
To rub over a Whimsical Life
There's no one Folly is so true,
As that very bad Bargain a Wife;
We'er just like a Mouse in a Trap,
Or Vermin caught in a Gin;
We Sweat and Fret, and try to Escape
And Curse the sad Hour we came in.

*Pills to Purge Melancholy* – Vol. I

*XXVII*

─────── AIR VI.   What shall I do to show how much I love her? ───────

Virgins are like the fair flower in its lustre,
Which in the garden enamels the ground;
Near it the Bees in play flutter and cluster,
And gaudy Butterflies frolick around.
But, when once pluck'd, 'tis no
        longer alluring,
To Covent Garden 'tis sent, (as yet sweet,)
There fades, and shrinks, and grows
        past all enduring,
Rots, stinks, and dies, and is
        trod under feet.

What shall I do to show how much I love her,
How many millions of sighs can suffice?
That which wins other hearts ne'er can move her,
Those common methods of Love she'll despise:
I will love her more than Man
        e'er lov'd before me,
Gaze on her all the Day, and melt all the Night,
'Till for her own sake at
        last she'll implore me,
To love her less to pre-
        serve our delight.

*Pills to Purge Melancholy* – Vol. **IV**

This song is by Purcell and comes from his opera *Dioclesian*.

─────── AIR VII.   Oh London is a fine Town. ───────

Our Polly is a sad slut!
        nor heeds what we have taught her.
I wonder any man alive
        will ever rear a daughter!
For she must have both hoods and gowns,
        and hoops to swell her pride,
With scarfs and stays, and gloves and lace;
        and she will have men beside;
And when she's drest with care and cost,
        all-tempting, fine and gay,
As men should serve a Cowcumber,
        she flings herself away.

Oh London is a fine Town,
        and a gallant City,
'Tis Govern'd by the Scarlet Gown,
        come listen to my Ditty;
This City has a Mayor,
        this Mayor is a Lord,
He Governeth the Citizens
        upon his own accord;
He boasteth his Gentility,
        and how Nobly he was born;
His Arms are three Ox-heads,
        and his Crest a Rampant Horn.

*Pills to Purge Melancholy* – Vol. **IV**

"Peggy Ramsay" is another name for this air, which was used for many popular songs in the eighteenth century.

—————— AIR VIII.   Grim King of the Ghosts, &c. ——————

*Can Love be controul'd by advice?*
*Will Cupid our mothers obey?*
*Though my heart were as frozen as Ice,*
*At his flame 'twould have melted away.*
*When he kist me so closely he prest,*
*'Twas so sweet that I must have comply'd:*
*So I thought it both safest and best*
*To marry, for fear you should chide.*

*Despairing besides a clear stream,*
*A Shepherd forsaken was laid;*
*And whilst a false Nymph was his Theme,*
*A Willow supported his Head:*
*The Winds that blew over the Plain,*
*To his Sighs with a Sigh did reply;*
*And the Brook in return for his Pain,*
*Ran mournfully murmuring by.*

*Pills to Purge Melancholy* – Vol. VI

This verse from "Collins Complaint" by Nicholas Rowe is much closer to the sense of the song as Gay used it than another version called "The Lunatick Lover: Or, The Young Man's Call to Grim King of the Ghosts for Cure". Gay must have known a song by Berkeley, "The Modest Question":

*Can love be controul'd by advice,*
*Can Madness and Reason agree:*
*O Molly who'd ever be wise,*
*If Madness is loving of Thee.*

The tune was also adapted by Purcell to "Hail to the Myrtle Shades" in *Theodosius* (1860).

—————— AIR IX.   O Jenny, O Jenny, where hast thou been. ——————

*O Polly, you might have toy'd and kist.*
*By keeping men off, you keep them on.*
*But he so teaz'd me,*
*And he so pleas'd me,*
*What I did, you must have done.*

*Oh Jenny, Jenny, where hast thou been?*
*Father and Mother are seeking for thee,*
*You have been ranting,*
*     playing the Wanton,*
*Keeping of Jockey company.*

*Pills to Purge Melancholy* – Vol. I

This is titled "The Willoughby Whim. A Scotch Song. In a Dialogue between two Sisters", words by D'Urfey. It is well known today as "Golden Slumbers Kiss Your Eyes".

*XXIX*

———————— AIR X.  Thomas, I cannot, &c. ————————

I, like a ship in storms, was tost;
Yet afraid to put in to Land;
For seiz'd in the port the vessel's lost,
Whose treasure is contreband.
The waves are laid,
My duty's paid.
O joy beyond expression!
Thus, safe a-shore,
I ask no more,
[My all is in my possession, possession,]
My all is in my possession.

Come, come, my Molly, come let us be jolly,
Since we are here met together;
My Mother's from Home, and we are alone,
Come let us be merry together;
I'll give you Rings,
          and Bracelets fine,
And other fine Trinkets, if you'll be mine.
O no, kind Sir,
          I dare not incline.
My Mother, she tells me I munnot, I munnot,
My Mother she tells me I munnot.

*The Dancing Master*

In Scotch collections it is set to "My mither says I mauna".


———————— AIR XI.  A Soldier and a Sailor. ————————

A Fox may steal your hens, sir,
A whore your health and pence, sir,
Your daughter rob your chest, sir,
Your wife may steal your rest, sir,
A thief your goods and plate.
[A thief your goods and plate.]
But this is all but picking,
With rest, pence, chest and chicken;
It ever was decreed, sir,
If Lawyer's hand is fee'd, sir,
He steals your whole estate.
[He steals your whole estate.]

A Soldier and a Sailor,
A Tinker and a Tailor,
Had once a doubtful strife Sir
To make a maid a Wife Sir
Whose name was buxome Joan,
Whose name was buxome Joan:
For now the time was ended,
When she no more intended
To lick her Lips at Man, Sir,
And gnaw the Sheets in vain, Sir,
And lie a Nights alone,
And lie a Nights alone.

*Pills to Purge Melancholy* – Vol. III

The similarity here is made more striking by the use of the word "sir" at the ends of the lines. In Volume VI there are two more settings under the title "The Battle Royal". The second of these bears the subtitle "The Saint turn'd Sinner, Or the Dissenting Parson's Text under the Quaker's Petticoats".

——————— AIR XII.   Now ponder well, ye parents dear. ———————

*Oh, ponder well! be not severe;*
*So save a wretched wife!*
*For on the rope that hangs my dear*
*Depends poor Polly's life.*

*Now ponder well, You parents dear*
*These words which I shall write;*
*A doleful story you shall hear*
*In time brought forth to light.*

*Pills to Purge Melancholy* (1709)

Also called "The Children in the Wood" and "The Norfolk Gentleman, his Will and Testament".

——————— AIR XIII.   Le printemps rappelle aux armes. ———————

*The Turtle thus with plaintive crying,*
*Her lover dying,*
*The Turtle thus with plaintive crying*
*Laments her Dove.*
*Down she drops quite spent\* with sighing*
*Pair'd in death, as pair'd in love.*

*Le printems, r'apelle aux armes,*
     *Couller mes larmes;*
*Le printems, r'apelle aux armes,*
     *a quel tourment,*
*Grand Dieu parmis, tant d'allarmes, epargnezmon,*
*Cher amant bis.*

*Spring invites, the Troops are going,*
     *let Tears be flowing,*
*Spring invites, the Troops are going,*
     *ah, cruel smart,*
*Midst alarming, dreadful harming,*
*Spare him Fate, who charms my Heart.*

*Pills to Purge Melancholy* – Vol. I

These are the original French words of "Chanson en Francais", with D'Urfey's translation. It is hard to believe that this flowing melody is called "Hark! the Trumpet Sounds to Arms" in Walsh and Hare's musical edition (1732). As an outstanding example of Gay's gift of matching words with music, notice the scale down on the word "drops" in his version.

\*The word "pent" in the text is evidently a typographical error.

*XXXI*

——————— AIR XIV.  Pretty Parrot, say, &c. ———————

| | |
|---|---|
| *Pretty Polly, say,* | *Pretty Parret say,* |
| *When I was away,* | *when I was away,* |
| *Did your fancy never stray* | *And in dull absence pass'd the Day;* |
| *To some newer lover?* | *What at home was doing;* |
| *Without disguise,* | *With Chat and Play,* |
| *Heaving sighs,* | *We are Gay,* |
| *Doating eyes,* | *Night and Day,* |
| *My constant heart discover.* | *Good Chear and Mirth Renewing;* |
| *Fondly let me loll!* | *Singing, Laughing all,* |
| *[Fondly let me loll!]* | *Singing Laughing all,* |
| *O pretty, pretty Poll.* | *like pretty, pretty Poll.* |

*Pills to Purge Melancholy* – Vol. V

This is listed as "A New Song. Translated from the French". A comparison here shows how little Gay did to the original to achieve a song which, though a bit fatuous, fits the situation perfectly. This is Macheath's first appearance.

——————— AIR XV.  Pray, fair one, be kind. ———————

| | |
|---|---|
| *My heart was so free,* | *Come Fair one be kind,* |
| *It rov'd like the Bee,* | *you never shall find,* |
| *'Till Polly my passion requited;* | *A Fellow so fit for a Lover;* |
| *I sipt each flower,* | *The World shall view,* |
| *I chang'd every hour,* | *my Passion for you,* |
| *[I sipt each flower,* | *The World shall view,* |
| *I chang'd every hour,]* | *my Passion for you,* |
| *But here ev'ry flower is united.* | *But never your Passion discover.* |

*Pills to Purge Melancholy* – Vol. IV

Titled "A Song Set by Mr. Leveridge Sung by Mr. Wilks in the Comedy call'd The Recruiting-Officer". Here in Gay's version are, as the Beggar assures the Player in the Prologue, "the Similes that are in all your celebrated Operas: . . . the Bee, . . . the Flower, &c".

─────────── AIR XVI.   Over the hills and far away. ───────────

*Were I laid on Greenland's coast,*
*And in my arms embrac'd my lass;*
*Warm amidst eternal frost,*
*Too soon the half year's night would pass.*
*Were I sold on Indian soil,*
*Soon as the burning day was clos'd,*
*I could mock the sultry toil,*
*When on my charmer's breast repos'd.*
*And I would love you all the day,*
*Every night would kiss and play,*
*If with me you'd fondly stray*
*Over the hills and far away.*

*Jockey was a bonny Lad,*          (2nd verse)
*And e'er was born in Scotland fair;*
*But now poor Jockey is run mad,*
*For Jenny causes his Despair;*
*Jockey was a Piper's Son,*
*And fell in Love while he was young:*
*But all the Tunes that he could play,*
*Was, o'er the Hills, and far away,*
*'Tis o'er the Hills, and far away,*
*'Tis o'er the Hills, and far away,*
*'Tis o'er the Hills, and far away,*
*The wind has blown my Plad away.*

*Pills to Purge Melancholy* – Vol. V

Many verses have been set to this fine old air, but this one contains some of the lines most familiar now. The tune and an adaptation of the original words were used by Farquhar in *The Recruiting Officer*, Act II, Scene iii.

─────────── AIR XVII.   Gin thou wert mine awn thing. ───────────

*O what pain it is to part!*
*Can I leave thee, can I leave thee?*
*O what pain it is to part!*
*Can thy Polly ever leave thee?*
*But lest death my love should thwart,*
*And bring thee to the fatal cart,*
*Thus I tear thee from my bleeding heart!*
*Fly hence, and let me leave thee.*

*Gin thou wer't my e'ne Thing*
*I wou'd Love thee I wou'd Love thee*
*Gin thou wer't my e'ne Thing*
*So Dearly I wou'd Love thee*
*I wou'd take thee in my Arms*
*I'de Secure thee From all Harms*
*Above all Mortals thou has Charms*
*So Dearly do I love thee.*

*Orpheus Caledonius*

Titled "Scotch Song" (1700), this genuinely touching air was also used by Francesco Geminiani (1687-1762) for a theme with variations for violin solo. An amusing anecdote tells of a German musicologist who, in a study of *The Beggar's Opera*, took the other meaning of the word "gin" and translated the title of this song as "Schnaps, du bist meine einzige Freude".

──────── AIR XVIII. O the broom, &c. ────────

The Miser thus a shilling sees,
Which he's oblig'd to pay,
With sighs resigns it by degrees,
And fears 'tis gone for aye.
The Boy thus, when his Sparrow's flown,
The bird in silence eyes;
But soon as out of sight 'tis gone,
Whines, whimpers, sobs and cries.

O ye Broom, ye bonny, bonny Broom,
The Broom of Cowden-knows,
I wish I were at Hame again
To milk my Daddys Ews.
How blyth ilk Morn was I to see
The Swain come o'er the Hill.
He skipt ye Burn and flew to me,
I met him with good Will.

*Orpheus Caledonius*

In spite of the Scotch setting, the tune is undoubtedly old Irish, and makes a touching end to Act I as Macheath and Polly part, "Looking back at each other with fondness; he at one door, she at the other".

──────── AIR XIX. Fill ev'ry glass, &c. ────────

Fill ev'ry glass, for wine inspires us,
And fires us
With courage, love and joy.
Women and wine should life employ.
Is there ought else on earth desirous?

Que chacun remplisse son verre,
Pour boire
    a nos trois Generaux,
Par tout ou marchent ces Heros,
Ils menent a pres eux la victoire,
Que chacun remplisse son verre,
Pour boire a nos trois Generaux.

Fill every Glass, and recommend 'em,
We'll drink our
    three Generals Healths at large,
For whereso'er these Heroes march,
Conquest renown'd is sure t'attend 'em;
Fill every Glass, and recommend 'em,
We'll drink our three Generals Healths at large.

*Pills to Purge Melancholy* – Vol. **I**

"A drinking Song, in praise of our Three fam'd Generals" (Marlborough, Eugene, and D'Auverquerque), translated from the French by D'Urfey.

————— AIR XX.    March in *Rinaldo*, with Drums and Trumpets. —————

(Let us take the road)

The tune is from Handel's opera, produced in 1711. A comparison with the original shows differences in the melody which would arise from a faulty rendering of the tune by memory. In *Rinaldo* the tune is used only instrumentally, so there are no earlier lyrics except in a tavern setting of the tune, "Let the waiter bring clean glasses", which had quite a vogue before Gay used it.

————— AIR XXI.    Would you have a young Virgin, &c. —————

*If the heart of a man is deprest with cares,*
*The mist is dispell'd when a woman appears;*
*Like the notes of a fiddle, she sweetly, sweetly*
*Raises the spirits, and charms our ears.*
*Roses and lillies her cheeks disclose,*
*But her ripe lips are more sweet than those.*
*Press her,*
*Caress her,*
*With blisses,*
*Her kisses*
*Dissolve us in pleasure, and soft repose.*

*Would ye have a young Virgin of fifteen Years,*
*You must tickle her Fancy with sweets and dears,*
*Ever toying, and playing, and sweetly, sweetly,*
*Sing a Love Sonnet, and charm her Ears:*
*Wittily, prettily talk her down,*
*Chase her, and praise her, if fair or brown,*
*Sooth her,*
*    and smooth her,*
*And teaze her,*
*    and please her,*
*And touch but her Smicket, and all's your own.*

*Pills to Purge Melancholy* – Vol. I

The second verse begins "Do ye fancy a Widow well known in a Man?", and the third, "Do you fancy a Punk of a Humour free, That's kept by a Fumbler of Quality". Both of these give the same kind of advice.

————— AIR XXII.    Cotillon. (Youth's the season made for joys) —————

*The Dancing Master*

This is indeed a French tune, as requested by Macheath of the harper. It was known as "Tony's (or Zoney's) Rant". It appears in LeSage's *Télémaque* as "Ma commère quand je danse".

*XXXV*

——————————— AIR XXIII.   All in a misty morning. ———————————

Before the barn-door crowing,
The Cock by Hens attended,
His eyes around him throwing,
Stands for a while suspended.
Then one he singles from the crew,
And cheers the happy Hen;
With how do you do, and how do you do,
And how do you do again.

All in a misty Morning,
cloudy was the Weather,
I meeting with an old Man,
was cloathed all in Leather,
With ne'er a Shirt unto his Back,
but Wool unto his Skin;
With how do you do? and how do you do?
and how do you do agen?

*Pills to Purge Melancholy* – Vol. IV

The tune is also called "The London Prentice", "The Friar and the Nun", and "A Beggar got a Beadle". The last two lines are the refrain for all stanzas. These verses have survived in modern Mother Goose collections.

——————————— AIR XXIV.   When once I lay with another man's wife. ———————————

The Gamesters and Lawyers are jugglers alike,
If they meddle your all is in danger:
Like Gypsies, if once they can finger a souse,
Your pockets they pick,
    and they pilfer your house,
And give your estate to a stranger.

At Winchester was a wedding,
The like was never seen,
'Twixt lusty young Ralph of Reading,
And bonny black Bess of the green;
The Fiddlers did crowd before,
Each lass was as fine as a queen,
A hundred there were and more,
For all the country came in.

*Pills to Purge Melancholy* – Vol. I

This is titled "The Winchester Wedding" and is also known as "The King's Jig". The tune of the version given here is not the same as the one used by Gay.

*XXXVI*

——————— AIR XXV.   When first I laid siege to my Chloris. ———————

*At the Tree I shall suffer with pleasure,*
*At the Tree I shall suffer with pleasure,*
*Let me go where I will,*
*In all kinds of ill,*
*I shall find no such Furies as these are.*

*When first I lay'd siege to my Chloris,*
*When first I lay'd siege to my Chloris,*
*Cannon Oaths I brought down,*
*To batter the Town,*
*And boom'd her with amorous Stories.*

*Pills to Purge Melancholy* – Vol. VI

——————— AIR XXVI.   Courtiers, Courtiers think it no harm. ———————

*Man may escape from rope and gun;*
*Nay, some have out-liv'd the Doctor's pill:*
*Who takes a woman must be undone,*
*That Basilisk is sure to kill.*
*The Fly that sips treacle is lost in the sweets,*
*So he that tastes woman, woman, woman,*
*He that tastes woman, ruin meets.*

*Courtiers, Courtiers, think it no harm,*
*That silly poor Swains in Love should be;*
*For Love lies hid in Rags all torn,*
*As well as silks and Bravery:*
*For the Beggar he loves his Lass as dear,*
*As he that hath Thousands, Thousands, Thousands,*
*He that hath Thousand Pounds a year.*

*Pills to Purge Melancholy* – Vol. IV

In the D'Urfey version, the first four lines are set to music which is identical with the opening of "Cold and Raw" (Air III—If any wench Venus's girdle wears), but for the last three lines the tune corresponds to Gay's version.

——————— AIR XXVII.   A lovely Lass to a Friar came. ———————

*Thus when a good huswife sees a Rat*
*In her trap in the morning taken,*
*With pleasure her heart goes pit a pat,*
*In revenge for her loss of bacon.*
*Then she throws him*
*To the Dog or Cat,*
*To be worried, crush'd and shaken.*

*A lovely lass to a Friar came,*
*To confess in the morning early;*
*In what my Dear was you to blame,*
*Now tell to me sincerely,*
*I have done Sir*
    *what I dare not name,*
*With a man that loves me Dearly.*

*The Musical Miscellany* – Vol. VI

## —— AIR XXVIII. 'Twas when the Sea was roaring. ——

How cruel are the traytors,
Who lye and swear in jest,
To cheat unguarded creatures
Of virtue, fame, and rest!
Whoever steals a shilling,
Thro' shame the guilt conceals:
In love the perjur'd villain
With boasts the theft reveals.

'Twas when the Sea was roaring
With hollow blasts of wind;
A damsel lay deploring
All on a rock reclined
Wide o'er the rolling billows
She cast a wistful look;
Her head was crown'd with willows
That tremble o'er the brook.

The original version of this song was also by John Gay, and appeared in an earlier stage piece called *The What d'ye Call It* (1715). The tune is attributed to Handel. It is also called "The Melancholy Nymph". The song tells the sad story of the waiting maiden who sees her drowned lover come floating back.

*(Courtesy of the New York Public Library)* Drexel Collection

——————— AIR XXIX.   The Sun had loos'd his weary teams. ———————

*The first time at the looking-glass*
*The mother sets her daughter,*
*The Image strikes the smiling lass*
*With self-love ever after.*
*Each time she looks, she, fonder grown,*
*Thinks ev'ry charm grows stronger:*
*But alas, vain maid, all eyes but your own*
*Can see you are not younger.*

*The Sun had loos'd his weary Team*
*And turn'd his Steeds a grazing;*
*Ten fathoms deep in Neptunes Stream*
*His Thetis was embracing.*
*The Stars they tripp'd in the Firmament,*
*Like Milkmaids on a May-day;*
*Or Country Lasses a Mumming sent,*
*Or School Boys on a Play-day.*

*Pills to Purge Melancholy* – Vol. I

The original soon abandons this lofty tone and goes on to tell of a hurried trip for a midwife. It is also called "The Winchester Christening". "Lorenzo you amuse the Town" is another setting, in Vol. VI of D'Urfey.

——————— AIR XXX.   How happy are we, &c. ———————

*When you censure the age,*
*Be cautious and sage,*
*Lest the Courtiers offended should be:*
*If you mention vice or bribe,*
*'Tis so pat to all the tribe;*
*Each cries—That was levell'd at me.*

*How happy are we,*
*Who from thinking are free,*
*That curbing Disease of the Mind:*
*Can indulge every Tast,*
*Love where we like best,*
*Not by dull Reputation confin'd.*

*Pills to Purge Melancholy* – Vol. VI

The heading in D'Urfey reads: "A Song, in the Play call'd the Ladies Fine Aires: Sung by Mr. Pack, in the Figure of a Bawd".

——————— AIR XXXI.   Of a noble Race was Shenkin. ———————

*Is then his fate decreed, Sir?*
*Such a man can I think of quitting?*
*When first we met, so moves me yet,*
*O see how my heart is splitting!*

*Of noble Race was Shinking,*
*The Line of Woen Tudor,*
*But her Renown is fled and gone,*
*Since cruel Love pursu'd her.*

*Pills to Purge Melancholy* – Vol. II

──────── AIR XXXII. (You'll think, e'er many days ensue) ────────

This air and Air XXXVII (Cease your Funning) are the only two tunes not named by Gay. The first part of Air XXXII corresponds closely to "In the Fields in Frost and Snows" which appears in Vol. II of *Pills to Purge Melancholy*. The second part differs considerably. The tune has been used for the song "How should I your true love know", sung by Ophelia in *Hamlet*.

──────── AIR XXXIII. London Ladies. ────────

*If you at an Office solicit your due,*
*And would not have matters neglected;*
*You must quicken the Clerk*
　　*with the perquisite too,*
*To do what his duty directed.*
*Or would you the frowns of a lady prevent,*
*She too has this palpable failing,*
*The perquisite softens her into consent;*
*That reason with all is prevailing.*

*Ladies of London, both Wealthy and Fair,*
*Whom every Town Fop is pursuing;*
*Still of your Purses*
　　*and Persons take care,*
*The greatest Deceit lies in Wooing.*
*From the first Rank of Beaux Esprits,*
*Their Vices therefore I discover,*
*Down to the basest Mechanick degree,*
*That so you may chuse out a lover.*

*Pills to Purge Melancholy* – Vol. **II**

──────── AIR XXXIV. All in the Downs, &c. ────────

*Thus when the Swallow, seeking prey,*
*Within the sash is closely pent,*
*His consort with bemoaning lay,*
*Without sits pining for th' event.*
*Her chatt'ring lovers all around her skim;*
*She heeds them not (poor bird)*
　　*her soul's with him.*

*All in the Downs the fleet was moor'd,*
*The streamers waving in the wind,*
*When black-eyed Susan came aboard,*
*Oh! where shall I my true love find!*
*Tell me, ye jovial sailors, tell me true,*
*If my sweet William sails*
　　*among the crew.*

*The Musical Miscellany* – Vol. **IV**

The original words are also by Gay, and were called "Sweet William's farewell to Black-eyed Susan". Carey, Haydon, Leveridge, and Sandoni wrote music to Gay's original. This tune is supposed to be by P. G. Sandoni, a harpsichord maker and husband of the famous singer Cuzzoni.

*X L*

───── AIR XXXV. Have you heard of a frolicksome ditty. ─────

*How happy could I be with either,*
*Were t'other dear charmer away!*
*But while you thus teaze me together,*
*To neither a word will I say;*
*But tol de rol, &c.*

*Give ear to a frolicsome ditty,*
*Of one who a wager would lay,*
*He'd pass every watch in the city*
*And never a word would he say,*
*But dal dera, rara, dal dara, &c.*

*Popular Music of the Olden Time*

The original ballad was called "The jolly Gentleman's frolick; or, The City Ramble". Another title for the same song was "Give ear to a frolicsome ditty; or, The Rant".

───── AIR XXXVI.   Irish Trot. (I'm bubbled) ─────

An air by this name appears in *Dancing Master*. It is also known as "Hyde Park".

───── AIR XXXVII.   (Cease your funning) ─────

This is the other of the two airs not named by Gay. A considerable amount of research on this song has shed a little light on its origin, as well as its further career after *The Beggar's Opera*. The source of the song must have been a dance of some kind. Two dances under the titles "None so pretty" and "Constant Billy" show up as Morris dances, with almost exactly the same melody as the first part of the song. The second part, however, is completely different. Chappell, in *National English Airs* (p. 131), states: "It is traditionally said to have been composed expressly for the opera by a lady, a friend of the poet". It could very likely be that the original inspiration of the song was a dance, and the second part was newly composed. This conjecture could also explain Air XXXII.

An arrangement by Beethoven of "Cease your funning" appears in the *Collected Works* No. 5 in Series 24 among the 12 Scotch songs, with the words exactly as Gay wrote them, but with no credit for authorship. (In the same series of songs "Auld Lang Syne" is found.)

*X L I*

—————————— AIR XXXVIII.   Good-morrow, Gossip Joan. ——————————

*Why how now, madam Flirt?*
*If you thus must chatter,*
*And are for flinging dirt,*
*Let's try who best can spatter;*
    *Madam Flirt!*
*Why how now, saucy Jade;*
*Sure the wench is tipsy!*
*How can you see me made*
*The scoff of such a Gipsy?*
    *Saucy Jade!*

*Good morrow Gossip Joan,*
*Where have you been a walking;*
*I have for you at home,*
*A Budget full of talking,*
    *Gossip Joan.*
*My Sparrow's flown away,*
*And will no more come to me;*
*I've broke a Glass to day,*
*The price will quite undo me,*
    *Gossip Joan.*

      *Pills to Purge Melancholy* – Vol. VI

—————————— AIR XXXIX.   Irish Howl. ——————————

*No power on earth can e'er divide*
*The knot that sacred Love hath ty'd.*
*When parents draw against our mind,*
*The true-love's knot they faster bind.*
*Ho hora in ambora*
  *ho an ho derry hi an hi derry*
  *hoo hoo derry derry derry Derry ambora.*

*Remember Damon you did tell,*
*In Chastity you lov'd me well,*
*But now alas I am undone,*
*And here am left to make my Moan.*
*Haugh hora in amboora,*
*Ho and ho derry, hi an hi derry,*
*Hoo hoo derry, derry, derry derry amboora.*

      *The Dancing Master*

—————————— AIR XL.   The Lass of Patie's Mill. ——————————

*I like the Fox shall grieve,*
*Whose mate hath left her side,*
*Whom Hounds, from morn to eve,*
*Chase o'er the country wide.*
*Where can my lover hide?*
*Where cheat the wary pack?*
*If Love be not his guide,*
*He never will come back!*

*The Lass of Patties Mill,*
  *sa bony blith and gay;*
*In spight of aw my skill,*
  *she stole my heart away;*
*When tedding of the hay,*
  *bare headed on the green,*
*Love midst her locks did play,*
  *and wanton'd in her een.*

      *Orpheus Caledonius*

## ——————— AIR XLI.  If Love's a sweet passion, &c. ———————

*When young at the bar you*
  *first taught me to score,*
*And bid me be free of*
  *my lips, and no more;*
*I was kiss'd by the Parson,*
  *the Squire, and the Sot:*
*When the guest was departed,*
  *the kiss was forgot.*
*But his kiss was so sweet, and*
  *so closely he prest,*
*That I languish'd and pin'd till*
  *I granted the rest.*

*If Love's a sweet Passion,*
  *why does it Torment?*
*If a bitter, oh tell me!*
  *whence comes my content;*
*Since I suffer with Pleasure*
  *why should I complain,*
*Or grieve at my Fate, when*
  *I know 'tis in vain?*
*Yet so pleasing the Pain is,*
  *so soft is the Dart,*
*That at once it both wounds me,*
  *and tickles my Heart.*

*Pills to Purge Melancholy* – Vol. **III**

The air by Henry Purcell appears in his opera *The Faerie Queen* (1692).

## ——————— AIR XLII.  South-Sea Ballad. ———————

*My love is all madness and folly,*
*Alone I lye,*
*Toss, tumble, and cry,*
*What a happy creature is Polly!*
*Was e'er such a wretch as I!*
*With rage I redden like scarlet,*
*That my dear inconstant Varlet,*
*Stark blind to my charms,*
*Is lost in the arms*
*Of that Jilt, that inveigling Harlot!*
*Stark blind to my charms,*
*Is lost in the arms*
*Of that Jilt, that inveigling Harlot!*
*This, this my resentment alarms.*

*Change Alley's so thin*
  *that a man may now walk,*
*And if he'l but listen*
  *may hear himself talk,*
*For Since the Suppression*
  *of Bubbles in June,*
*Those clamorous Catches*
  *are quite out of tune.*
*No more of the Hubbles,*
  *nor Bubbles, we See,*
*But all the whole Nation*
  *attends the South Sea.*

*The Dancing Master*

This song of the same name, to a different tune, is one of many ballads contemporary to the South Sea Bubble.

─────────── AIR XLIII.  Packington's Pound ───────────

*Thus Gamesters united in*
*    friendship are found,*
*Though they know that their industry*
*    all is a cheat;*
*They flock to their prey at the Dice-box's sound,*
*And join to promote one another's deceit.*
*But if by mishap*
*They fail of a chap,*
*To keep in their hands, they each other entrap.*
*Like Pikes, lank with hunger, who*
*    miss of their ends,*
*They bite their companions, and*
*    prey on their friends.*

*My Masters and Friends, and good*
*    People draw near,*
*And look to your Purses, for*
*    that I do say;*
*And tho' little Money, in them do you bear.*
*It cost more to get, then to lose in a day.*
*You oft have been told,*
*Both the young and the old;*
*And bidden beware of the Cut-purse so bold:*
*Then if you take heed not, free*
*    me from the Curse,*
*Who both give you warning, for,*
*    and the Cut-purse.*

To an air by Thomas Paggington, a musician to Henry VII, Ben Jonson
had set "a gentle Admonition both to the Purse-cutter, and the Purse-bearer"
in his play *Bartholmew Fair, A Comedy. Acted in the Year 1614.* This ballad appears
in *Pills* Vol. IV as "The Cut-Purse", and has also been called "A Caveat for
Cut-purses". Among numerous other ballads written to "Paggington's Pound"
were: "The Crafty Maid of the West", "Oxford in Mourning", "Rome in an
Uproar", "The Maiden's Longing", and Gay's own "Newgate's Garland".

─────────── AIR XLIV.  Lillibulero. ───────────

*The modes of the Court so common are grown,*
*That a true friend can hardly be met;*
*Friendship for interest is but a loan,*
*Which they let out for what they can get.*
*'Tis true, you find*
*Some friends so kind,*
*Who will give you good counsel themselves to defend.*
*In sorrowful ditty,*
*They promise, they pity,*
*But shift you for money, from friend to friend.*

*Ho! brother Teague, dost hear de decree?*
*Lilli burlero, bullen a la,*
*Dat we shall have a new deputie,*
*    Lilli burlero, bullen a la.*
*Lero, lero,*
*    lilli burlero,*
*    Lilli bullero, bullen a la,*
*Lero, lero,*
*    lilli burlero,*
*Lilli bullero, bullen a la.*

*Pills to Purge Melancholy* – Vols. **II** and **IV**

The occasion for this verse was the appointment of General Talbot to the Lieutenancy of Ireland in 1687. Bishop Burnet in his *History of His Own Time* states: "The whole army and at last the people, both in the city and country, were singing it, and perhaps never had so slight a thing so great an effect". Numerous songs were set to this air, all having a strong Protestant bearing. It has been said that this ballad sang James out of three kingdoms. "Lilliburlero, etc." seem to be mere nonsense words. No meaning can be discovered for them. Countless verses have been set to the tune, which was also used by Henry Purcell.

──────────── AIR XLV.  Down in the North Country. ────────────

*What Gudgeons are we men!*
*Ev'ry woman's easy prey.*
*Though we have felt the hook, agen*
*We bite, and they betray.*
*The bird that hath been trapt,*
*When he hears his calling mate,*
*To her he flies, again he's clapt*
*Within the wiry grate.*

*Down in the north Country*
*As ancient reports do tell*
*There lies a famous Country Town*
*Some cal it merry wakefield*
*And in this Country Town*
*A Farmer there did dwell*
*Whose Daughter would to market go*
*Her treasure for to sell.*

*The Dancing Master*

Called "The Farmer's Daughter of Merry Wakefield".

──────────── AIR XLVI.  A Shepherd kept sheep, &c. ────────────

*In the days of my youth I could*
*  bill like a Dove, fa, la, la, &c.*
*Like a Sparrow at all times*
*  was ready for love, fa, la, la, &c.*
*The life of all mortals in kissing should pass,*
*Lip to lip while we're young—then the*
*  lip to the glass, fa, la, &c.*

*A Shepherd kept sheep on a*
*  hill so high, Fa la la &c*
*And there came a pretty maid*
*  passing by, Fa la la &c*
*Shepherd, quoth she, dost thou want e'er a Wife*
*No by my troth I'm not*
*  weary of my life, fa, la, la, &c.*

*Pills to Purge Melancholy* – Vol. V

The tune, however, is different.

*XLV*

──────── AIR XLVII.   One evening having lost my way. ────────

I'm like a skiff on the Ocean tost,
Now high, now low, with each billow born,
With her rudder broke, and her anchor lost,
Deserted and all forlorn.
While thus I lye rolling and tossing all night,
That Polly lyes sporting on seas of delight!
Revenge, revenge, revenge,
Shall appease my restless sprite.

One evening having lost my way,
By chance I came into a Wood,
Soll had been very hot that Day,
I under a Covert stood,
Long time I had not tarried there,
Before I heard a russling Nigh,
A Female voice said stay my Dear
The Man cry'd Zoons not I.

*The Dancing Master*

Also known as "Do you fancy a Semstress brisk and gay", and "Walpole, or The Happy Clown".

────── AIR XLVIII.   Now Roger, I'll tell thee, because thou'rt my son. ──────

When a wife's in her pout,
(As she's sometimes, no doubt)
The good husband as meek as a lamb,
Her vapours to still,
First grants her her will,
And the quieting draught is a dram.
Poor man! And the quieting draught is a dram.

And now my dear Robin,
    since thou art my son,
I'll give you good counsel in life,
Go haste thee away
    and make no delay
And I'll warrant I'll get thee a wife.

──────── AIR XLIX.   O Bessy Bell, &c. ────────

A curse attends that woman's love
Who always would be pleasing.
The pertness of the billing Dove,
Like tickling, is but teazing.
What then in love can woman do?
If we grow fond they shun us.
And when we fly them, they pursue:
But leave us when they've won us.

O Bessy Bell and Mary Gray,
They were twa bonny lasses,
They bigg'd a bower on yon Burn-brae
And theek'd it o'er wi' rashes.
Fair Bessy Bell I lov'd yestreen
And thought I ne'er cou'd alter;
But Mary Gray's twa pawky een,
They gar my fancy falter.

*Orpheus Caledonius*

—————————— AIR L.   Wou'd Fate to me Belinda give. ——————————

Among the men, Coquets we find,
Who court by turns all woman-kind;
And we grant all their hearts desir'd,
When they are flatter'd, [when they are flatter'd,
    when they are flatter'd,] and admir'd.

Wou'd Fate to me Belinda give,
With her alone I'd Chuse to Live,
Nor with her cou'd I more require,
Nor a greater, nor a greater,
    nor a greater Bliss desire.

*The Musical Miscellany* — Vol. I

—————————— AIR LI.   Come, sweet lass. ——————————

Come, sweet lass,
Let's banish sorrow
'Till to-morrow;
Come, sweet lass,
Let's take a chirping glass.
Wine can clear
The vapours of despair;
And make us light as air;
Then drink, and banish care.

Come Sweet Lass,
This bonny Weather,
    Let's together:
Come Sweet Lass,
Let's trip it on the Grass:
Ev'ry where,
Poor Jockey seeks his Dear,
And unless you appear,
He sees no Beauty here.

*Pills to Purge Melancholy* – Vol. III

—————————— AIR LII.   The last time I went o'er the Moor. ——————————

Hither, dear husband, turn your eyes.
Bestow one glance to cheer me.
Think with that look, thy Polly dyes.
O shun me not,—but hear me.
'Tis Polly sues.
'Tis Lucy speaks.
Is thus true love requited?
My heart is bursting.
Mine too breaks.
Must I,
Must I be slighted?

The last Time I came o'er the Moor,
I left my Love behind me;
Ye Pow'rs! what Pain do I endure,
When soft Ideas mind me?
Soon as the
    ruddy Morn display'd
The beaming Day ensuing,
I met betimes
    my lovely Maid,
In fit
    Retreats for Wooing.

*Orpheus Caledonius*

—————— AIR LIII.   Tom Tinker's my true love, &c. ——————

Which way shall I turn me—how
    can I decide?
Wives, the day of our death, are as
    fond as a bride.
One wife is too much for most
    husbands to hear,
But two at a time there's no
    mortal can bear.
This way, and that way, and
    which way I will,
What would comfort the one, t'other
    wife would take ill.

Tom Tinker's my true love, and
    I am his Dear,
And I will go with him his
    Budget to bear;
For of all the young Men he
    has the best luck,
All the Day he will Fuddle, at
    Night he will —
This way, that way,
    which way you will,
I am sure I say nothing that
    you can take Ill.

*Pills to Purge Melancholy* – Vol. VI

—————— AIR LIV.   I am a poor Shepherd undone. ——————

When my Hero in court appears,
And stands arraign'd for his life,
Then think of poor Polly's tears;
For ah! poor Polly's his wife.
Like the Sailor he holds up his hand,
Distrest on the dashing wave.
To die a dry death at land,
Is as bad as a watry grave.
And alas, poor Polly!
Alack, and well-a-day!
Before I was in love,
Oh! every month was May.

I am a poor Shepherd undone,
And cannot be Cur'd by Art;
For a Nymph as bright as the Sun,
Has stole away my Heart:
And how to get it again,
There's none but she can tell;
To cure me of my Pain,
By saying she loves me well:
And alass poor Shepherd,
Alack and a welladay;
Before I was in Love,
Oh every Month was May.

*Pills to Purge Melancholy* – Vol. VI

    The title is given as "The Distressed Shepherd". It is also known as "Hey,
ho, my honey".

─────────────── AIR LV.　Ianthe the lovely, &c. ───────────────

When he holds up his hand
　　arraign'd for his life,
O think of your daughter,
　　and think I'm his wife!
What are cannons, or bombs,
　　or clashing of swords?
For death is more certain
　　by witnesses words.
Then nail up their lips;
　　that dread thunder allay;
And each month of my life, [and each month
　　of my life]
　　will hereafter be May.

Ianthia the lovely,
　　the Joy of her Swain,
By Iphis was lov'd,
　　and lov'd Iphis again;
She liv'd in the Youth,
　　and the Youth in the Fair,
Their pleasure was equal,
　　and equal their Care;
No Time, no Enjoyment
　　their Dotage withdrew;
But the longer they liv'd, but the longer
　　they liv'd,
Still the fonder they grew.

*Pills to Purge Melancholy* – Vol. V

This same air appears in an arrangement by Haydn in Vol. II of Thomson's *Songs of Scotland* under the title "Mourn hapless Caledonia".

─────────────── AIR LVI.　A Cobler there was, &c. ───────────────

Our selves, like the Great,
　　to secure a retreat,
When matters require it,
　　must give up our gang:
And good reason why,
Or, instead of the fry,
Ev'n Peachum and I,
Like poor petty rascals, might hang, hang;
Like poor petty rascals, might hang.

A Cobler there was,
　　and he liv'd in a Stall,
Which serv'd him for Parlour,
　　for Kitchen, and Hall,
No Coin in his Pocket,
　　nor Care in his Pate,
No ambition had he,
　　nor Duns at his Gate:
Derry down, down, down, derry down.

*The Musical Miscellany* – Vol. II

The title: "The Cobler's End. Set by Mr. Leveridge". Also called "Derry Down", "Abbott of Canterbury", and "Death and the Cobler".

## —————— AIR LVII.  Bonny Dundee. ——————

*The charge is prepar'd; the Lawyers are met;*
*The Judges all rang'd (a terrible show!)*
*I go, undismay'd.—For death is a debt,*
*A debt on demand.—So, take what I owe.*
*Then farewell, my love—dear charmers, adieu.*
*Contented I die—'tis the better for you.*
*Here ends all dispute the rest of our lives,*
*For this way at once I please all my wives.*

*Where gott'st thou the Haver-mill bonack?*
*Blind Booby canst thou not see;*
*Ise got it out of the Scotch-man's Wallet,*
*As he lig lousing him under a Tree:*
*Come fill up my Cup, come fill up my Can,*
*Come Saddle my Horse, and call up my Man;*
*Come open the gates, and let me go free,*
*And shew me the way to bonny Dundee.*

*Pills to Purge Melancholy* – Vol. V

Titled: "Jockey's Escape from Dundee; and the Parson's Daughter whom he had Mow'd".

## —————— AIR LVIII.  Happy Groves. ——————

*O cruel, cruel, cruel case!*
*Must I suffer this disgrace?*

*Oh! happy, happy Groves,*
   *Witness of our tender loves;*
*Oh! happy, happy shade,*
   *where first our Vows were made.*

*Pills to Purge Melancholy* – Vol. IV

The above and the next eight airs are sung in snatches by Macheath as he endeavors to raise his spirits with brandy so that he can go bravely to the gallows.

## —————— AIR LIX.  Of all the girls that are so smart. ——————

*Of all the friends in time of grief,*
*When threatning Death looks grimmer,*
*Not one so sure can bring relief,*
*As this best friend a brimmer.*

*Of all the girls that are so smart,*
*There's none like pretty Sally,*
*She is the Darling of my Heart,*
*And she lives in our Alley.*

This is the famous "Sally in our Alley", words and music by Henry Carey.

———————————— AIR LX.  Britons strike home. ————————————

*Since I must swing,—I scorn,*
*I scorn to wince or whine.*

*To Arms to Arms to Arms to Arms*
*Your Ensigns strait display*
*Now, now, now, now*
*Set the Battle in array.*

Purcell wrote this air for the opera *Bonduca* (1695). It later became a national favorite like "Rule Britannia" and "God Save the King".

———————————— AIR LXI.  Chevy Chase. ————————————

*But now again my spirits sink;*
*I'll raise them high with wine.*

*Some Christian People all give Ear*
*Unto the Grief of us,*
*Caus'd by the death of three Children dear,*
*The which it happen'd thus.*

*Pills to Purge Melancholy* – Vols. III and IV

Titled: "Three Children Sliding on the Thames. Tune Chivy-Chase". This very old tune seems to have had an affinity for sad settings. The other versions are titled: "An Unhappy Memorable Song, of the Hunting in Chevy-Chase, between Earl Piercy of England, and Earl Dowglas of Scotland"; "A New Song, upon the Robin-red-breast's attending Queen Mary's Hearse in Westminster Abby"; "A Warning to all Custard Eaters".

———————————— AIR LXII.  To old Sir Simon the King. ————————————

*But valour the stronger grows,*
*The stronger liquor we're drinking.*
*And how can we feel our woes,*
*When we've lost the trouble of thinking?*

*In a humour I was of late*
*As many good fellows be;*
*To think of no matters of State,*
*But seek for good Company:*

*Pills to Purge Melancholy* – Vols. III and IV

Also called "The Reformed Drinker" and "A true Character of sundry Trades and Callings: or a new Ditty of Innocent Mirth."

──────────── AIR LXIII.   Joy to great Caesar. ────────────

*If thus—A man can die*
*Much bolder with brandy.*

*Joy to Great Caesar,*
*Long Life, Love and Pleasure;*
*'Tis a Health that Divine is,*
*Fill the Bowl high as mine is.*

*Pills to Purge Melancholy* – Vol. **II**

Titled: "The King's Health. Set to Farinel's Ground. In Six Parts". Farinel's Ground was the name under which the famous "Folies d'Espagne" was known in England. This tune has served countless composers: Frescobaldi, Corelli, Vivaldi, Marais, to name a few.

──────────── AIR LXIV.   There was an old woman, &c. ────────────

*So I drink off this bumper—*
*And now I can stand the test,*
*And my Comrades shall see,*
*that I die as brave as the best.*

*There was an Old Woman that had but one son,*
*And he had neither Land nor Fee:*
*He took great Pains, But got little Gains,*
*Yet fain a Landlord he would be.*

*Pills to Purge Melancholy* – Vol. **IV**

The tune is not the same.

──────────── AIR LXV.   Did you ever hear of a gallant sailor. ────────────

*But can I leave my pretty hussies,*
*Without one tear, or tender sigh?*

*Did you not hear of a gallant Sailor,*
*Whose Pockets they were lin'd with Gold.*

*Pills to Purge Melancholy* – Vol. **III**

──────────── AIR LXVI.   Why are mine eyes still flowing. ────────────

*Their eyes, their lips, their busses*
*Recall my love—Ah must I die!*

*Why are my Eyes still flowing,*
*Why does my Heart thus trembling move?*

*Pills to Purge Melancholy* – Vol. **II**

———————————————— AIR LXVII.   Green sleeves. ————————————————

*Since laws were made for ev'ry degree,*
*To curb vice in others, as well as me,*
*I wonder we han't better company*
*Upon Tyburn tree!*
*But gold from law can take out the sting;*
*And if rich men like us were to swing,*
*'Twou'd thin the land, such numbers to string*
*Upon Tyburn tree!*

*Alas! my love, you do me wrong,*
*To cast me off discourteously,*
*And I have loved you so long,*
*Delighting in your company.*
*Greensleeves was all my joy,*
*Greensleeves was my delight,*
*Greensleeves was my heart of gold,*
*And who but Lady Greensleeves.*

*Pills to Purge Melancholy* – Vol. IV

The above is from *A Handful of Pleasant Delites* (1584) where the piece is entitled "A New Courtly Sonnet, of the Lady Greensleeves". Shakespeare refers to "Green Sleeves" in *Merry Wives* (Act II, Scene i, and Act V, scene v). This famous tune was used for many songs.

———————————— AIR LXVIII.   All you that must take a leap, &c. ————————————

*Would I might be hang'd!*
*And I would so too!*
*To be hang'd with you,*
*My dear, with you.*
*O leave me to thought! I fear! I doubt!*
*I tremble! I droop!—See, my courage is out.*
*No token of love?*
*See, my courage is out.*
*No token of love?*
*Adieu.*
*Farewell.*
*But hark! I hear the toll of the bell.*

*All you that must take*
*a leap in the dark,*
*Pity the Fate of*
*Lawson and Clark;*
*Cheated by Hope, by Mercy amus'd,*
*Betray'd by the sinful ways we us'd:*
*Cropp'd in our Prime*
*of Strength and Youth,*
*Who can but weep at*
*so sad*
*a Truth.*

*Pills to Purge Melancholy* – Vol. VI

Titled: "A Hymn upon the Execution of Two Criminals, by Mr. Ramondon" (1710). This was a very serious ballad written about two criminals who repented publicly before their hanging.

─────── AIR LXIX.   Lumps of Pudding, &c. ───────

*Thus I stand like the Turk,*
  *with his doxies around;*
*From all sides their glances*
  *his passion confound;*
*For black, brown, and fair,*
  *his inconstancy burns,*
*And the different beauties*
  *subdue him by turns;*
*Each calls forth her charms,*
  *to provoke his desires:*
*Though willing to all;*
  *with but one he retires.*
*But think of this maxim,*
  *and put off your sorrow,*
*The wretch of to-day,*
  *may be happy to-morrow.*

*My Mother she killed*
  *a good fat Hog,*
*She made such Puddings*
  *would choak a Dog;*
*And I shall ne'er*
  *forget till I dee*
*What lumps of Pudding*
  *my Mother gave me.*
*She hung them up*
  *upon a Pin,*
*The Fat run out and the*
  *Maggots crept in;*
*If you won't believe me you*
  *may go and see,*
*What lumps of Pudding*
  *my Mother gave me.*

*Pills to Purge Melancholy* – Vols II and VI

Also called "The Loyal Scot: Or, the King's New Health, to a Scotch Tune".